Ecological
Economics

THE GROUP OF GREEN ECONOMISTS

Ecological Economics

A PRACTICAL PROGRAMME FOR GLOBAL REFORM

ZED BOOKS

LONDON & NEW JERSEY

Translated by Anna Gyorgy

Ecological Economics: A Practical Programme for Global Reform was first published in German as *Die Grünen im Bundestag: auf dem Weg zu einer ökologischen-solidarischen Weltwirtschaft* by Bundesgeschäftesstelle der Grünen, Colmanstr. 36, 5000 Bonn in 1991.

First published in English by Zed Books Ltd, 57 Caledonian Road, London N1 9BU, UK and 165 First Avenue, Atlantic Highlands, New Jersey 07716, USA, in 1992.

Cover picture by Joker
Cover design by Andrew Corbett
Typeset by Photosetting and Secretarial Services, Yeovil, Somerset
Printed and bound in the UK by Billing and Sons Ltd, Worcester

ISBN 1 85649 069 6 hb
ISBN 1 85649 070 X pb

British Library Cataloguing and Publication Data
A catalogue record for this book is available from the British Library

Library of Congress Cataloging and Publication Data
US CIP is available from the Library of Congress

Contents

Foreword

Working in the Bundestag is rather like working in a hospital emergency ward. Parliamentary politics is defined by rapidly changing world and national events. There is little time to think through the long-range implications of the flood of legal changes on the agenda.

Consequently, in spring 1988, an interdisciplinary group was set up to formulate a coherent international economic and ecological policy programme, based on the cultural values developed by the social emancipatory movements active since the 1960s.

Most members of this group were either employees or MPs for the Green Party in Bonn. The Green Parliamentary Group, represented by some 47 MPs, managed to pool their financial resources, including their own salaries, to employ about 200 people, around half of whom were researchers. The Group of Green Economists was thus a small sub-section of the entire enterprise, working together on a daily basis, preparing parliamentary debates and legislative reform proposals on a range of economic policy and Third World issues.

Over a three-year period the group met for lengthy discussions on alternate Friday afternoons. We were very lucky to have Dieter Bricke as our chief economist, co-ordinator and director. It was generous of the German Minister of Foreign Affairs, Dietrich Genscher to second a senior expert to the Greens for the duration of the entire project. Applying modern techniques of professional diplomacy to our co-operative work effort was a new and enriching experience that we recommend for similar efforts in the future.

During 1988 and 1989 we held a series of eight hearings in Bonn, to which we invited academics, policy experts and activists on key issues of foreign economic policy; each hearing brought together theory, policy and cultural aspects. By and large the topics covered are reflected in the different chapters of this book: international trade; consumer policy; tourism; finance and banking; the EC internal market and its relations to other economic regions in East, West and South; multinational corporations; environmental policy; and weapon production.

We aimed to integrate the women's perspective in each of these topics, rather than relegate feminism to a special chapter. A similar approach was taken regarding the environment. While there is a chapter dealing with international environmental policy, we apply an analysis of structural ecology to each issue. We see this integrative approach as one of our primary contributions.

A second important innovation we pursued is the focus on the interaction between economic policy (industrial country economics) and development (applied to the Third World and Eastern Europe). Patterns of consumption and production in the North and the social and economic structure in the South together contribute to the destruction of the environment. Therefore, an ecological perspective requires an integrated interactive view quite aside from the necessity to formulate development policies and environmental policies. We summarized this idea by replacing the traditional approach of foreign economic policy in the national interest with the search for national policies in the interest of global survival.

Two events were crucial to harnessing the project to real-life activism. In 1988 we became actively involved in the IMF-World Bank campaign and congress in West Berlin. In one way or another most of us are involved in movements for peace, the environment, women's rights, Third World solidarity, East-West relations, support for the homeless in urban centres and multicultural life in Germany. It was therefore logical to participate in preparing this campaign.

In March 1990 we organized an international meeting of experts and activists in Bonn. The purpose of this was to discuss the first written draft of our policy programme with scholars, politicians and representatives of the emancipatory movements worldwide. In both instances we received many valuable comments and criticism for our work. We also renewed and extended our contacts and were encouraged to continue.

While in the first round, we each took charge of one chapter, the second and third versions received substantial reformulations. Finally, we each sponsored one chapter, that is, took primary responsibility, but everyone wrote or rewrote sections of the entire piece. We felt that leaving some rough edges in the text was justified. There are several places where, in the end, we simply agreed to disagree and then point out that several approaches appear equally valid.

The Appendices at the end of the book were commissioned by the group. Christa Wichterich wrote Women of the South; Wolfgang Kessler, the piece on raw material trade; Klaus Seitz is the author of Appendix 3, on Agricultural Trade; Christian Busold wrote on Drug Traffic; and Appendix 5, on Arms Exports, was written by Dietmar Pietsch.

For valuable suggestions and criticisms we thank: Elmar Altvater; Tamas Bauer (CSFR/Frankfurt); Manfred Busch; Frank Bracho (Venezuela); Reinhard Doleschal; Christopher Flavin (USA); Wilhelm Hankel; Hansjörg Herr; Hazel Henderson (USA); Wilhelm Höynck; Milan Horacek; Thomas Kampffmeyer; Kitazawa Yoko (Japan); Ingo Klein (East Germany); Vladimir Kollontai (Soviet Union); Martin Khor (Malaysia); Otto Kreye; Christopher Layton (UK); Reinhard Loske; Ueli Maeder (Switzerland); Masha Madörin (Switzerland); Klaus Milke; P. Pallangyo (Ethiopia); Udo Pollmer; Elzbieta Rawicz-Oledzka

(Poland); Jürgen Riedel; Halo Saibold; Angelina Sörgel; Otto Schily; Heffa Schücking; Klaus Voy; Ernst-Ulrich von Weizsäcker; Elisabeth Weber; Herbert Wulf (Sweden).

The English edition, finalized in 1990 and the first half of 1991, was a somewhat separate project. It turned out that a professional translation was inadequate for getting our ideas across to an international audience. A mix of idioms and non-standard language from economics, politics and movement-related terminology required substantial changes and revisions. We therefore formed a team composed of Denise Taylor, who did the first literal translation, Anna Gyorgy and Claudia Dziobek who edited the translation and Nancy Folbre, economics professor at the University of Massachusetts in Amherst, who read and commented on the manuscript for us. Anna Gyorgy's work deserves special mentioning. With her background as environmental activist and author, and her experience of living as a foreigner in Germany, she contributed much to the final product. She helped organize the international meeting of experts and carefully edited the final version of the text with each one of the Group of Green Economists. This was complicated by the fact that most of us are now engaged in new jobs and living at various places in and outside of Germany.

During the preparation of this work, the political map – of Europe – and the world – has changed dramatically. For us it is ever clearer that East-West, North-South, and economic relations in the West can no longer be responsible or successful without first developing a comprehensive concept of world economics based on ecology and solidarity. We hope that this book is a useful contribution.

Preface: down to earth economics

Bringing our own ecology back into tune with the ecology of the rest of nature will be the most important (and the hardest) challenge ever faced by the human species. How it might be accomplished is the sole topic of the debates around the 1992 United Nations Conference on Environment and Development in which governments are being confronted with evidence, unprecedented in quantity and quality, that current patterns of human activity are seriously undermining the power of the planet's biosphere to assure a life-supporting environment.

Already, in private if not in public, many governments admit our predicament is not merely a blip in the otherwise smooth path of human development but the inevitable consequence of a dangerously unsustainable trend. The evidence of strong links between collapsing global ecosystems, uneconomic economies, disintegrating communities and spiritual disenchantment is increasingly difficult to ignore.

But governments have an exquisite dilemma. Their chances of staying in power depend largely on their ability to deliver a strong economic performance. Yet to do so they rely most heavily on the very human activities which cause the most environmental damage – the oil, petrochemical and metal industries, agriculture, public utilities, road-building, transport and mining for example.[1]

So far, their attempts to resolve this dilemma have focused principally on 'better management' of the resources and services of the environment. Unfortunately, recent massive expenditure on international research into climate change, for example, has revealed two problems with this approach. First, there is greater uncertainty than we thought about the mechanisms affecting climate, and secondly, we are more ignorant than we thought about how the natural world functions. This is hardly a satisfactory basis for subjecting the ecological wisdom of the environment to the comparatively juvenile discipline of human management techniques.

But slowly (albeit far too slowly) it is dawning on governments, industry and citizens alike that the environment actually knows all there is to know about managing ecological balance; that it is we who need to study nature's management techniques and apply them to our own activities. This book forms part of a growing effort to apply ecological principles to human economic activities, an effort which over the last decade has been spearheaded by Greens in several countries.

Ecological Economics points out that current economics is more about the career of cash than about the real source of all our wealth – the natural environment. The primacy of cash, not only as a means of exchange but as the key indicator of human well-being, has ensured that economic efficiency is achieved by off-loading as many costs as possible on other factors in the economy, notably the environment and people. It has also ensured the unfair advantage of value-added goods over primary products in increasingly global markets where prices are set according to relative power as much as supply and demand. It has spawned the crazy notion that we could create wealth through debt. The effect of this new era of what might well be called 'uneconomic growth' is bitterly summed up by Emil Salim, Indonesia's Environment Minister, who recently pointed out that today his country needs to cut down three times more trees to buy a tractor than it did in the 1970s. Furthermore, because debt has so distorted the global financial system, Indonesia also contributes to the net transfer of $50 billion which takes place from the poor to the rich each year.

No wonder the newly liberated East European economies look askance at the efforts of the West to hook them into the ruthless dynamic of this world economy. No wonder they are concerned about the motives behind offers to help them exploit their considerable natural resources. Without radical changes to the rules of the game, the Second World quite rightly fears it will be forced to join the Third World.

But it does not have to be this way. There is an alternative. For a long time, Greens have argued that although an ecological economy would use very recognizable mechanisms it would have radically different goals and strategies. Green economics challenges key assumptions of traditional economics (as practised in East and West Europe): that the economy must always produce *more* and that man-made capital is an adequate substitute for natural capital. Surely the goal of any human economy based on even a shred of justice must be to provide *enough* for everyone? Can a Disneyland theme park ever substitute for the productive agricultural land it has covered?[2]

In an ecological system, the often fragile individual parts gain their strength from their relationships within that system. In fact, the greater the diversity of an ecological system and the greater the number of links between it and other neighbouring systems the stronger it is. This principle, diversity combined with interdependency, is the key to how a green economy might look. The overall economic dynamic would not be towards single-strand connections with the largest market possible, a heroically misnamed strategy known as the comparative advantage of the free market (how can the advantages of cocoa-bean growing be compared with those of computer manufacture?) but towards the smallest possible market. Only in small markets can buyers and sellers assemble the required information to set *fair* prices, limit the distortion that relative power imposes on markets and feed ecological and social justice into the market mechanism.

Once the objective of developing the most locally diverse (self-reliant) economies possible is accepted as a policy goal, other mechanisms for developing ecologically sound patterns of human economic activity make a lot more sense. The move of taxation policy away from earned to unearned income, for example, would mean energy and resource taxation can encourage local production for local use in order to save transportation costs and thus reduce emissions of carbon dioxide, the main greenhouse gas. Activities favouring re-use, restoration and recycling of materials can become cost effective (and create employment) rather than costly, as at present. A hierarchy of levels of monetary policy becomes logical rather than heretical, with local banks able to offer incentives which keep money working locally.[3]

Bringing economic decision-making close to the people who are not only going to pay for the decision but live the consequences of it makes it more likely that the decision will be a good one – for the environment and for people. And as we move into difficult and uncertain times, building ecologically sound (diverse and interdependent) local economies and the confident democratic institutions essential to their sustainability, is likely to be the only way we can avoid mass human misery and the migrations which may well herald a rise of authoritarian regimes.

It is becoming clear that governments of all persuasions are feeling the constraint their national political boundaries impose on their search for solutions to problems which present themselves at global and community level. To change our economies, they say, is impossible unless others change simultaneously – to go it alone would be catastrophic. It therefore becomes very important that they use global institutions like the UN and its agencies to give a lead in affecting the sort of global change which will allow local change to flourish.

In fact, perhaps the most critical policy breakthrough the United Nations Conference on Environment and Development could make would be to announce the publication of a new set of indicators of human well-being, ones which encompass social and environmental factors as well as economic ones. Running such indicators *prominently and parallel* with traditional (mainly cash) indicators would, more than anything else, highlight the direction an ecologically sustainable economy should take.[4]

A similar exercise could be undertaken with new methods of compiling national accounts. The present system, set up after the end of the Second World War (and primarily concerned with paying for it) is both environmentally and socially distorting. For example, trees in the ground have no value, but once cut for timber they do; and the majority of women's work, critical to rich and poor economies alike, is arbitrarily excluded from the calculations.[5]

The time for chronicling our dilemma in ever more minute detail must surely be over. Working out where we want to go, by looking first hand at human and environmental well-being rather than through the prism of cashflows, and by accounting with ecological accuracy for our activities, will be central to the debate amongst governments, the GATT, industry and citizens on how we might literally bring our manner of doing business with each other down to earth. *Ecological Economics: A Practical Programme for Global Reform* makes a most valuable contribution to that debate.

Sara Parkin

Notes

1. Jan Tinbergen and Hueting Roefie, 'GNP and market prices: wrong signals for sustainable economic success that mask environmental destruction' in Robert Goodland, Herman Daly and Salah El Serafy (eds) *Environmentally Sustainable Economic Development: Building on Brundtland* (1991 World Bank).
2. Daly, Herman and John Cobb, *For the Common Good* (1989) Beacon Press, Boston.
3. Kemball-Cook, David, Mallen Baker and Chris Mattingly (eds) *The Green Budget* (1990) Green Print.
4. Anderson, Victor, *Alternative Economic Indicators* (1991) Routledge, London.
5. Waring, Marilyn, *If Women Counted* (1989) Macmillan, London.

Introduction

Green principles for reordering the global economy

In early 1990 United States Ambassador to Germany, Vernon Walters, commented on the radical changes in Eastern Europe and the Soviet Union: 'What functions is obvious, the principle of the free market economy.'

What bothers us about Vernon Walters and the political and economic circles he speaks for is how the market is presented as the ultimate goal and is transformed into an expression of freedom. What this means above all is unlimited freedom for capital transactions and multinational enterprises. Yet the path of these financiers is marked by crisis regions, which, when profits looked better elsewhere, have been left behind with high unemployment, poverty and environmental damage.

What this 'freedom' means is that banks can earn a pot of gold in Third World or Eastern European credits. But millions of people are not part of this freedom: those who can barely eke out an existence at starvation level because their countries are burdened by interest and loan repayments or those who – in order to survive – are forced to destroy their natural environment.

Apparently the 'free market economy' is also not concerned when dictators in Third World countries trample on the human rights of their citizens to meet the deregulation requirements of the International Monetary Fund.

It seems to us that the collapse of the centralized 'plan and command' economy in the Eastern bloc countries does not prove that the Western industrial countries can just keep going along as before. We think, on the contrary, that continuing along the current path of industrial development prevents the solution of many problems facing humanity. The blind trust in industrial growth strategies inherent in both systems and derived from a mechanistic philosophy of progress has been the motor for the destruction of the earth's atmosphere, oceans and forests and the contamination of soil and groundwater.

Free-traders and plan economists share the unreflective ideology of 'the more, the better' and the greedy handling of nature. Responsibility also lies with today's free market apologists, the followers of the naïve market economists of the eighteenth century who, without regard for global social consequences or the preservation of the planet, assume that the unrestrained pursuit of individual self-interest brings prosperity to all. The reality of a global world with colossal potential for production and destruction has by now overtaken this hypothesis. If we want to survive we need a new model – East *and* West, North *and* South.

Our approach to international economics is no longer oriented towards 'partial analyses', but is of necessity 'holistic'. The increasing impoverishment of the Third World – a problem which to this day has been relegated by 'world economists' to being a problem for charitable welfare organizations – in combination with the approaching climate catastrophe, threatens the existence of global society. An alternative ecological management of the economy based on solidarity demands political far-sightedness, social sensibility and long-term economic calculation. It requires thinking based on global ecological cycles, from the careful handling of resources to the responsible utilization of waste. Such an approach is often directly opposed to short-term, business-oriented, cost-benefit considerations.

Growing up with the prospect of life-long poverty and suffering also forces people to develop short-term survival strategies, resulting in the destructive exploitation of tropical forests or 'voluntary' import of toxic waste from industrial states in order to make money. The extremely unequal concentration of wealth within the Third World aggravates the problem. The wealthy recklessly conduct business assuming that if catastrophe strikes they can take off for Florida or Western Europe.

Meanwhile, in the Western industrial states a form of superficially understood environmental protection has been promoted into a basic social consensus. No large corporation – whether it manufactures vehicles or chemicals or is a bank – fails to open its financial report without a long discourse on the responsible treatment of nature. But we all know that a 50 per cent reduction in waste emission coupled with a doubling of production is no long-term solution. Copying the failure of Western industrialization, which several developing countries in Asia are 'successfully' doing, is not ecologically sustainable on a global level.

Our rejection of the free trade doctrine is not a plea for protectionism. Protectionism is often simply the by-product of unlimited trade, where the weaker partner is forced to reach for this last straw. The measures we support to safeguard economically weaker regions would allow them to enter the market in the first place.

We reject standard ideological conclusions in which all contradictions are miraculously resolved. We recognize the need to develop, take on and support concrete, meaningful actions and strategies and in the course of this to continuously analyse successes and failures. As explained in the foreword, our approach is twofold. On the one hand we are working from the foreign-economic dimension of an ecological and social restructuring of industrial society. On the other hand we develop a holistic perspective on Third World politics, leaving classical approaches to development policy behind.

Both perspectives lead to a fundamental critique of the maximization of consumption, world market integration and export dependence. In the course of this work we have integrated both approaches into a Green concept for global economic development. This concept is characterized by four guiding principles:

1. self-reliant development through domestic and regional orientation;
2. ecological balance;
3. solidarity and equalization of development opportunities;
4. democratization of the global economy and protection of human rights.

Self-reliant development through domestic and regional orientation

For too long, 'progress' has meant modernization; so has what the West calls 'development'. We believe, however, that national and global economic policies that destroy the environment for present and future generations, and cause social injustice, can no longer be defined as development. They must be recognized as exploitation.

Our new concept of development recognizes the existence of diverse cultures and lifestyles. It attempts to secure the basic needs of each country's population. It seeks the greatest possible alignment of historically differing life chances, taking into account the ecological stress-bearing capacity of the planet.

Such development cannot be gauged by such quantitative measures as growth in the volume of world trade or gross national product. We can no longer accept economic concepts that measure success by increased exports or income and investment improvements without considering that much of the world's population lives and works outside the monetarized economy.

We believe that qualitative development goals must be defined. For us, economic growth is not a goal in itself, but is at best a partial result of the development process. The current fixation on growth is responsible for failed development in many parts of the world. In our opinion, an independent development process requires a well-planned policy of selective growth and contraction.

Self-reliance means having a domestic and regional rather than a world market orientation. This approach uses economic and social resources to meet basic needs, or for ecological and social restructuring.

Domestically oriented development is often falsely accused of striving for national autarky – unlimited sovereignty – or complete dissociation from the world market. This is not our aim. It would be naïve, if not disastrous, to reject the advantages of national and international divisions of labour.

Self-reliant development does not call for specialized division of labour at any price. It aims to integrate economic processes into socially meaningful local or regional economic contexts. Its clarity and comprehensibility are essential prerequisites for securing democratic control and responsible action. According to this concept, regional and domestic boundaries may be defined by geography or history. They do not have to correspond to national borders.

We are striving for self-reliant development of economically weaker states, despite the fact that present power relationships stand in the way. Such independent development is possible only if the rich industrial states adopt a foreign economic policy based on solidarity and voluntary restraint. From this perspective, the radical economic changes in central and eastern Europe actually offer great opportunities for countries there and worldwide. The first step in overcoming global economic and military blocs can be taken with the forthcoming Conference on Security and Co-operation in Europe (CSCE). The danger is, however, that these chances will be consciously wasted by efforts to expand the influence of NATO and the EC into the east.

Ecological balance

Today's global ecological problems clearly show that safeguarding the natural endowment of our planet must be key to the shaping of global economic relations. Ecological policies are essential for efficient economic policies. Ecological policy is, however, more than environmental policy. Ecological policy-making requires a redefinition of the relationship between humankind and nature. This applies to individual groups and cultures to differing degrees. Two systems, that of nature and that of society, must relate closely so that humans and nature can survive over time.

A redefinition of the relationship between humans and nature must result in new regulation of resource use and the stress on the environment. This approach can be called 'structural environmentalism'.

We advocate that the World Charter for Nature adopted by the UN General Assembly in 1982 become internationally binding with full judicial authority. This Charter contains a comprehensive record of obligations for the moderate and frugal handling of natural resources, and regulates the current monitoring of ecosystems.

In addition, valuable natural areas and ecosystems must be protected against economic exploitation. As the 'heirs of humankind' and part of a growing environmentally responsible international community, we want to see a World Park Antarctica and the remaining primeval forests protected as part of the 'Heritage of Mankind'.

We call for an international climate convention for the protection of the earth's atmosphere that can set effective limits on industrial and related emissions. Individual countries should be able to set stricter limits if they so choose.

To halt the further destruction of our planet, international trade bans are urgently necessary – for example on toxic waste, atomic technology, or pesticides banned in industrialized countries.

Far-reaching restrictions must be imposed on international tourism to reduce environmental damage and the destruction of cultural identity.

Finally, we call for the establishment of an International Fund for the Environment to pay for global environmental programmes. This international fund should be supported by contributions totalling approximately one per cent of all countries' gross national product. A central instrument for raising the money must be a global energy tax. For the time being, the industrial states –which up to this point have been both the main cause and the beneficiaries of failed development – must raise most of the funds needed to restructure the global economy ecologically.

Solidarity and equality of development opportunities

Social equity between North and South cannot be achieved through conventional development policies. Free-market economics and conservative policies support the idea of 'deregulating poverty'. Under the slogan originally coined in progressive circles – 'from help to self-help' – development policies under conservative leadership have increasingly left the poor alone with their problems.

We believe that the chances for dignity and development in the Third World can be improved only on the basis of fundamentally altered global economic conditions.

Self-reliant development of Third World nations – and this also applies to former Comecon countries – can only be achieved if forced integration into the world market ceases to be the primary goal. There is tremendous pressure, especially on highly indebted countries, to increase exports so as to earn foreign exchange to pay the interest on international debts. Our most central demand in respect to the creditor banks and states is, therefore, a comprehensive global cancellation of debt. The organization of debt cancellation should be discussed at an international conference on debt. As an intermediate step we demand an immediate moratorium on interest and repayment obligations.

Our qualitative concept of development is based on self-reliance, not primarily the transfer of capital. Third World countries automatically gain greater financial leeway when they receive better terms of trade. Still, in view of the net capital transfer from South to North, and their increasingly asymmetrical development, we feel that transfer payments from industrial states to Third World countries are necessary.

Basically the phrase 'to take less is better than to give more' should apply to the North. This means reorienting the economic development of the industrial states, considerably reducing our societies' demands for resources from southern countries.

A more equitable alignment of economic levels of development between North and South and among industrial states themselves requires an internationally binding economic and monetary mechanism that gradually dismantles the structural balance of payment surpluses and credit positions of wealthy countries. An example of this would be a progressive penalty interest payment on current account surpluses. This was actually proposed by John Maynard Keynes during discussions over the founding of the IMF in the 1940s.

The global economy and human rights

Today's capitalist world market takes little consideration of democratic or human rights. Transnational corporations increasingly determine global market relations and thus the development of entire countries. Their decisions often undermine the policies of democratically elected governments.

The transnationals' grip on the world is increasing, and they play off the peoples of different countries against each other when it comes to social and environmental questions. These corporations are therefore at the centre of our political critique. Above all, in the spirit of the principles of non-violence and decentralization, which we support, the power of the large banks and international weapons manufacturers must be reduced.

Only the democratization and decentralization of economic power can guarantee sufficient global fairness of distribution over the long-term and thereby secure world peace. We thus support efforts to create opportunities for effective co-determination and participation within transnational corporations. We also support the activities of consumer organizations, 'critical stockholders' and critical union members, and their attempts to network globally. We demand binding global codes of conduct for multinational corporations and effective anti-trust laws at the United Nations level.

In our opinion United Nations agreements on political, civil, social and cultural rights and related conventions of the International Labour Organization (ILO) or other special UN organizations, are of utmost importance for democratically sound global economic policies.

The most important building block of an ecological economy based on solidarity is a reordering of international financial relationships. We have mentioned the need for an international conference on debt to organize comprehensive debt cancellation. Beyond this, further dramatic changes are necessary to open new development opportunities for Third World countries.

Financial co-operation should shift from the bilateral to multilateral level. This is the only way meaningfully to focus the funds for North-South capital transfer.

The European Monetary System (EMS) must go beyond a European Monetary Fund and be further developed into a federalistic global monetary system that can integrate other regional monetary alliances.

The IMF's structure and decision-making should be democratized and the organization limited to financing short-term balance of payment deficits. We also support converting the World Bank Group into decentralized, non-profit-oriented fund structures in order to make well-directed, regionally useful and appropriate aid policies possible. We advocate 'taming' private international financial currents, by international regulation of the banks and financial markets, targeted taxation of speculation and strengthened control of the stock markets.

We propose the establishment of a UN World Economic Council analogous to the World Security Council. This body should meet regularly and co-ordinate functions, instead of the yearly World Economic Summit of the seven most powerful industrial states. The Council should agree on guidelines for economic and monetary policies.

Most importantly, the Council should be monitored in order to avoid or correct persistent balance of payment inequalities or social and environmental dumping practices. The rights and responsibilities of the World Economic Council must be decided at a UN Convention for an Ecological Global Economy Based on Solidarity.

Finally, we demand that the break-up of the military blocs and a new European order of peace be grounded economically in a new all-European economic order. This process could be linked to the existing economic areas – the European Community (EC), European Free Trade Association (EFTA) and the former Comecon states. It should strengthen their co-operation and finally lead to a new form of economic community. This community should surmount all borders and blocs, and should be guided by ecological values based on solidarity.

The European Council would be well-suited to become the institutional centre of the proposed integration process. Economic and environmental co-operation could be strengthened within the European Council on the basis of democratic equality and human rights.

The development of a unified Europe that can secure peace and overcome military blocs will require great effort and financial investment. Realizing this, we want to point out the danger of Eurocentrism. The great need for investment and restructuring in the countries of central and eastern Europe threatens to absorb all of Europe's energies. Urgent problems in the Third World could be forgotten. The Green Party wants an integrated, unified Europe that sees itself as part of one world, with special responsibility for the environment and social justice in all parts of the world.

We are convinced that the concepts outlined in this work are well-suited to be the basis for an internationally co-ordinated global economic and monetary policy. Of course, we do not evaluate our proposals only on the basis of what can be accomplished here and now. Rather we seek to present the first steps towards solutions that could be realized given that the corresponding political will existed. The stimulation and organization of this will is the task of Green politics. We must help forge coalitions at both national and international levels that will increase the chances for realizing an ecological global economy based on solidarity.

Our approach begins with the demands of widely differing social and environmental movements in the Third World and at home: grass-roots groups and religious organizations, unions, environmental groups, feminist and Third World solidarity groups, farmers' and consumers organizations. Further networking and focusing of their demands and energies, which can be observed in the successful example of the IMF campaign of 1988 and in the organization of coalitions such as The Other Economic Summit (TOES), speed the building of oppositional powers to the ruling global economic order.

In this sense Green foreign economic policies turn the previous maxims of all foreign policy upside-down. For us it is no longer international politics in the national interest, but national politics in the international interest.

1. Some basic principles for an ecological economy in one world

The ideology of free trade

In most countries of the Second and Third World attempts at 'catch-up industrialization' have failed. The attempt to repeat the economic miracles of industrialization without questioning the existing international division of labour has led to poverty, enormous indebtedness and a steady decline in the supply of essential goods.

Foreign debts of poor countries amount to $1.3 trillion. The debt service on these alone amounts to between six and seven per cent of their gross national products, and up to two-thirds of their people live in poverty. Eight hundred million people around the world live below the minimum subsistence level. One African in four suffers from hunger and endemic malnutrition.

Stringent economic austerity programmes imposed by the International Monetary Fund (IMF) have led to civil war-like situations in many countries. Farmers whose basis of subsistence is destroyed become economic refugees. Even according to the moderate criteria of the UN High Commissioner for Refugees, there were 15 million refugees in 1989. The International Red Cross estimate that there are as many as 500 million so-called environmental refugees worldwide.

Against this background of destructive global processes and ever more crass differences in living conditions between countries and population groups, it seems to us that an open, rational discourse on the reordering of the global economy is urgently needed. This discussion is of course no substitute for political action – it must accompany it.

The free-trade concept is repeatedly used by vested interests to legitimate capitalistic structures in the present world market rather than to help solve urgent problems. We believe there is an alternative: the concept of an ecological economy in one world. By 'one world' we mean that such an economy must be based on international solidarity, and a global approach. Both theoretical critique and historical experience show that more emphasis on 'free-trade 'welfare' only benefits the welfare of stronger nations, if that. This results from the industrial states' selective interpretation of the free-trade doctrine. They only demand the liberalization of trade in products where they enjoy comparative advantages – and call this international competitiveness.

Selective free-trade principles also apply to capital versus labour. While wealthy countries support deregulation of foreign investment (freedom to repatriate the profits), they vehemently oppose the right of workers to move to where work is. It is no coincidence that a restrictive immigration law in West Germany is coming into effect at the same time that controls on international capital transactions are being lifted.

The Green Party presented a political and economic concept for domestic economics in the Federal Republic of Germany in the 1986 programme, 'Reshaping Industrial Society'. This programme presents existing options for building an ecological economy based on solidarity in our country. It spells out what is possible if policy-makers stop running for cover behind so-called constraints. The *Umbauprogram* ('Reshaping Programme') presents economically feasible measures to tackle the most important problems facing Germany today – mass unemployment, poverty and environmental destruction. Its policy suggestions emphasize economic democracy and the economic and social equality of women.

The Green economic programme challenged the 'world market integration' ideology that overshadows all policy debates in Germany. 'World market integration' is considered the undisputed road to success by the public and

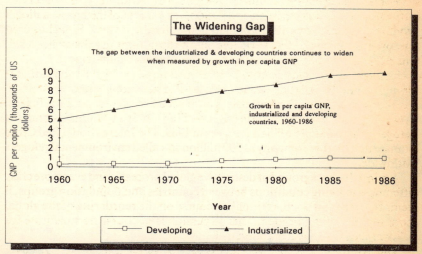

Source: UNICEF, *The State of the World's Children*. New York 1980, p.70

by so-called economic experts, despite obvious and persistent social and economic dislocations.

Economic growth, measured in terms of gross national product and export surpluses, continues to be the main measuring stick of success and 'achievement' in the global economic context. The negative dislocations are blamed on the insufficient realization of free-trade principles. The establishment concludes that prosperity can be increased and maintained only by abolishing international trade barriers.

Growth of volume of World Commodity Export and Production according to chief commodity groups (average variation in per cent)

	1970-80	1983-89	1987	1988	1989
World exports	5	6	5.5	8.5	7
Agriculture	4.5	3	6.5	5	4
Mining	1.5	4	2	6	4.5
Manufacturing	7	7.5	6.5	10	8
World output	4	4	3	4.5	4
Agricultural products	2	2	0.5	0.5	4
Mining products	2.5	2.5	1	5.5	2
Manufacturers	4.5	5	4.5	6.5	5

Source: GATT secretariat, Gent 1990

It cannot be denied that raising social and environmental standards in an open economy creates certain competitive disadvantages for products competing with other goods produced under less socially and environmentally sound conditions. However, it is wrong to claim that these 'disadvantages' inevitably threaten economic wealth. The high social standards of West Germany or Sweden, and in some areas Japan's partial role as environmental model, have in no way led to capital flight, 'capital strike' (refusal to invest), or economic decline – the dangers that interested parties complain about.

West Germany in particular enjoys a number of competitive advantages, including geographic location, a fully developed infrastructure, a highly qualified and over-disciplined work force. And furthermore, a gradual elimination of the chronic export surpluses is urgently needed from both a domestic and an international perspective.

Preaching the unqualified trust in the self-healing capabilities of the market and asserting the effectiveness of deregulation and liberalization is mainly political rhetoric. In reality, state intervention is the rule, in the form of subsidies for exports, duties on agricultural goods and import quotas. Many examples of state intervention are never publicly debated or decided upon, for instance in the field of monetary policy, which is one of the keys to the German export boom.

Thus the historically outdated ideology of so-called free trade must be openly attacked. This does not mean that in place of an unlimited world market integration we picture Germany as an autarkic state. Such a concept is doomed to failure.

The social sciences have almost always served the interests of the ruling elites and supplied them with appropriate conclusions. Economics is no exception. More than 150 years ago David Ricardo, one of the founders of foreign trade theory, invented the 'Ricardo Theorem' to explain the advantage of free trade between two countries (England and Portugal), correctly pointing out the actual importance of the existing political power structure. In doing so, he placed himself at the ideological services of Great Britain, then a rising world power, which forced militarily inferior Portugal to make specific trade concessions.

Today's refined variant, the so-called 'factor proportion theorem', is still the basis of prevailing foreign trade theory. This theory's policy conclusions in favour of free trade are hailed, while unrealistic assumptions, theoretical inconsistencies and the empirically proven negative results are either condoned or ignored.

The subjective interests behind this economistic concept need to be exposed. The Green Party constituency does not adopt the viewpoint of multinational corporations, banks or their academic allies. We define our interests differently – as citizens who want a world where responsible production and consumption determine priorities. A world that will remain habitable for the generations that follow us. We support the interests of emancipatory movements of farmers, producers, consumers, women, the unemployed and the socially disadvantaged.

A realistic utopia

We see 'ecological economics in one world' as a realistic utopia. This concept is indispensable, because it encourages each of us to participate in shaping a humane and ecological world. It is also a political weapon against free-trade policies that, especially in crisis situations, could pave the way for totalitarian and racist world views ('eco-dictators' for example).

It is good to know that today numerous political groups and organizations exist that can be encouraged and mobilized by such a concept. Nevertheless, drafting an alternative concept for the world economy does not by itself lead to its political realization. This will finally be determined by the actual power structures.

Instead of replacing binding beliefs and ethical values with the devastating economistic philosophy of 'deregulation', we are striving to regulate the world market by international agreements based on ethical principles. They could form the judicial basis of those emancipatory political concepts mentioned above. We see that in Western industrial societies and some countries of the Second and Third World such concepts are increasingly replacing the mechanistic free-trade paradigm.

We can see greater moral and technical possibilities for moving from egocentric, nationalistic and power-oriented economic behaviour to global economic behaviour oriented towards responsibility and solidarity. With this comes the basis for a viable new system of world economic responsibility capable of simultaneously taking into account economic, environmental and social perspectives. Key to the principles presented in the introduction is – based on humankind's painful experience – the worldwide recognition of human rights and the rights of nature.

The conditions for the implementation of a world economic concept based on these principles are more favourable than is often assumed. After the Second World War, the United Nations incorporated a worldwide guarantee of human rights into its objectives in the form of the International Charter of Human Rights and in the Civil Rights Agreement of 1976. These have become enforceable international law. They are noteworthy for guaranteeing social, economic and cultural rights, including independent rights for women and children.

These human rights agreements must still be expanded by legal conventions on the basis of the International Charter of Rights of Nature from 1982. It should also be noted that so-called 'human rights of the third generation', especially those of development, and the right to employment are still excluded from international treaties and economic legislation in individual states.

The world's churches are pointing out with increasing urgency that one hope for overcoming the fundamental global economic crisis lies in individual efforts at voluntary self-restraint. To us this means that individuals, especially those living in the industrial states, should practise voluntary self-restraint at all levels of society. Given the almost universal acceptance of the materialistic production-consumption model, the situation is an enormous political challenge.

Those who want to satisfy not just basic material needs but also the non-material needs of all members of global society from all cultures, must supplement current political and economic standards up to now considered absolute, such as economic growth, division of labour and competition, with additional political categories. In addition to economic criteria, environmental and social – in other words humane – criteria must be given equal consideration in economic policy discussions. Humane regulation must take the place of economic deregulation.

In the future, politicians who determine world economic policy must be judged by how effectively they secure basic needs throughout the world, realize the political self-determination of all, especially minorities, and work for the lasting preservation of our natural environment.

The rules of international competition must be embedded in a politically determined framework. Only if the market forces are firmly placed in a socially desired normative system can the mechanism of competition play its role as an instrument for improving quality-comparisons of goods and services. Only in such a setting does competition act as an automatic control of individual and national aspirations for power. From our experience with market economies, we know that even then the allocative functions of markets can be only partially realized. Nonetheless, competition clearly works better than distribution-management in centrally planned economic systems.

Democratization of economic relations

The international implementation of human rights and the rights of nature requires a dehierarchization of economic relations. In a world economic order based on solidarity, both excessive corporate and imbalanced national powers must be replaced by democratically legitimated institutions with the power to impose sanctions.

The investment power of international oligarchies and transnational corporations currently needs to be placed under constitutional limitations within a world economic order, similar to the way in which monopolized state power was controlled by constitutional limitations and the separation of powers in the modern state. This is necessary because large companies use their economic power to undermine democratically legitimated economic policies at national as well as international level.

The anchoring of international rights of co-determination, and other steps towards internal corporate democracy, create openness on all levels of production. They also provide the necessary conditions for responsible behaviour of producers and consumers. Only a global economic policy with popular democratic control and involvement can bring economic motives – such as the interests of capital holders in acquiring a return on their invested capital – into line with other social interests and needs. Only on this basis can individual firms' interests in utilizing their capital be compatible with other legitimate interests – environmental, consumer and workers'.

Rather than focusing on prices, interest and exchange rates, global economic policies should include criteria such as meaningfulness and appropriateness within an economic region. This principle would be violated when, for instance, the production of strawberries or tulips for export replaces food production at home, or if foreign exchange is earned by providing toxic waste dumps for industrial countries. Standard trade theory finds nothing wrong with that – a proof that something is wrong with standard theory!

An increasingly complex global economic system can no longer be safeguarded by the traditional hegemonic powers. It will be necessary for nation states to delegate part of their traditional sovereign rights either upwards (to multinational institutions) or downwards (to local populations and governments). Regional associations of states capable of worldwide co-operation are a possible first step for the upward delegation of power.

These regional economic communities need to agree on foreign trade strategies based on solidarity and on global economic institutions capable of effectively applying corrective strategies. Among other things, this will require the democratic development of international institutions and furthermore a radical reform of economic diplomacy and bureaucracy.

In a more advanced stage the United Nations or regional economic communities would be available as a supranational organizational framework, which will, however, require radical improvements in participation from below. Instruments for the downward delegation of national responsibilities are presented in our domestic programme.

In addition to the basic values of solidarity, ecology, and democracy, an ecological economy in one world must be secure. Our newspapers report almost daily on the sales of military equipment or even the deployment of troops. These are used to maintain the economic interests of industrial states. Yet global security today is no longer achievable with military methods, but must be won through disarmament and conversion, including the disarmament of economic might.

In the future, global conflicts will be avoidable only if the demand for world resources and energy is drastically reduced. The Gulf crisis was a dramatic case in point. The economically stronger states must take the first steps in this process of economic disarmament. Through such actions an ecological world economic order based on solidarity will also be key to safeguarding peace.

Co-operation based on solidarity

We can conclude that equal opportunity, distribution of wealth and sustainable development, global justice and the protection of nature can only be achieved if economic goals are embedded in an integrated complex of ethically motivated international agreements and treaties. Instead of prosperity for the few, we must strive for the welfare of all. The world market that is only seemingly 'free' must be replaced by an ecological world economic order based on solidarity.

A realistic utopia of this kind can be realized only if political majorities in the leading industrial countries take their survival into their own hands and carry out this task in co-operation with grassroots initiatives in the Second and Third Worlds. Then military technology will be converted into environmental technology. The global culture centred around capital will develop into a culture centred around life.

Ultimately it will be possible for an ecological world economic order based on solidarity to develop only through a progressive process in which joint political activities are carried out at the global level simultaneously with the promotion of local autonomy. In a dynamic and multipolar world economic system of this kind, individual and regional differences will be preserved and responsibility will be delegated in an upward direction only to the extent that is necessary to create ecological balance based on solidarity. The reconciliation of different interests will take place in this context on the basis of the commonly recognized Agreement on Human Rights and the Charter on the Rights of Nature.

2. Towards a global ecological policy

Extent and causes of environmental destruction

The global spread of industrial economic policies and lifestyles is exhausting the basic ecological wealth of our planet faster than it can be replenished. The natural resources on which the growing world population depends are in peril.

Every year the earth's deserts increase by six million hectares, almost 15 million acres. Year after year areas of productive agricultural land twice the size of Belgium are devastated. Each year three times as much land is so eroded that it is no longer commercially useful.

Almost every country in the world is confronted with water contamination or shortages and at least 1.5 billion people do not have clean drinking water. Surface and ground water is poisoned by nitrates and pesticides from agribusiness, and public and industrial waste water.

Then there is the problem of the 'treatment and disposal' of highly poisonous wastes produced by the industrial states. Some states take advantage of the foreign currency shortages and insufficient legal requirements in Third World and Eastern European countries to rid themselves of these problems cheaply.

Meanwhile the forests disappear. In Europe they are victims of environmental poisoning; in the tropics they are cut for commercial purposes. Their clear-felling is causing the largest loss of species of all time.

Five billion people inhabit this planet. It is estimated that by the year 2025 this population will double. Eighty per cent of the 10 billion will be born in Third World countries, in regions already experiencing massive hunger and suffering because of misdirected development, debts and dependencies.

With only a quarter of the world's population, the industrial nations consume far more energy, food and resources than so-called developing countries. Industrial states consume three-fourths of all energy produced and almost 80 per cent of all commercial fuels. The energy consumption of one citizen of the United States equals that of more than 160 Tanzanians or 900 Nepalis.

Paralleling this unequal consumption, the lion's share of climate-threatening gaseous emissions comes from the industrial nations. This is especially clear in the case of CFCs (chlorofluorocarbons) that destroy the ozone layer and make up some 17 per cent of the 'greenhouse gases' that create the climate-warming 'greenhouse effect'.

Worldwide, less than eight per cent of CFCs are produced by Third World countries. The pollution balance for carbon dioxide produced by burning fossil fuels is similar. The entire African continent is responsible for only 2.8 per cent of energy-related carbon dioxide (CO_2) emissions. The North American continent produces 28 per cent, Western Europe 15 per cent and the USSR and Eastern European countries together 21.5 per cent.

Most people in the Third World are victims of the industrialization model strived for by North and South. This has meant prosperity for the minority but unremitting poverty for the majority. As we discussed in Chapter 1, poverty and environmental destruction in Third World countries are the results of economically and politically unequal North-South relations. At the same time, the local elite in the Southern countries also play an important role, because its members underestimate the value of natural resources and trade them cheaply for modern technology and consumer goods.

In public debate the 'population explosion' in the Third World is often presented as the cause of poverty, impoverishment, and environmental destruction. Actually the causal relation is the opposite: it has been repeatedly proven that high population rates are a result of poverty. Poverty in turn forces people who are poor and hungry to seek ways to secure their survival regardless of the natural environment. This is the context in which environmental destruction, poverty and population growth are linked. Similarly, the Brundtland Report of the World Commission on Environment and Development argues against the ideological interpretation of population growth as the cause of poverty and environmental destruction.

Technocratic family planning as population control is supported by many industrialized countries today. It does not even begin to solve the actual problems. The programmes currently implemented by many international organizations and governments largely deny the relationship between poverty and population patterns. Furthermore, this so-called family planning reduces women to reproductive objects and forces them – often with economic pressure – to agree to sterilization or to use contraceptive methods dangerous to their health. This approach goes against the women's immediate self-interest of securing social security in a family network.

We insist that women be entitled to make their own reproductive decisions and control their lives and bodies. One prerequisite for achieving this is a development policy that is fair to women, that guarantees and secures basic needs, access to education and income-generating work. A fair development policy must also ensure greater access to political control and decision-making. Family planning must be embedded in this type of social and woman-specific development concept.

Well-informed politicians concerned with development have long known that increasing people's quality of life is the best population policy. When economic prosperity increases, birth rates fall. Achieving higher living standards with the same 'medicine' of economic growth that has been applied in the North is not, however, a viable option. There, the industrial model has managed to provide basic needs (and more) and halt population growth, but at high and ever-increasing ecological costs. The globalization of this model would quickly lead to global collapse, which is why a new model of development and a new definition of global wealth is urgently needed to replace the blind faith in industrial progress.

Current international eco-crisis management

Since the first UN Environment Conference in 1972 in Stockholm, ecology has secured a place on the international negotiating stage. Recent agreements include the 'Convention for the Protection of the Ozone Layer' adopted in Vienna, and the Basel 'Convention on the Control of Transboundary Movements of Hazardous Wastes and their Disposal'. In addition, there are treaties to regulate:

* the use of resources ('Convention on the Regulation of Antarctic Mineral Resource Activities' and the UN 'Convention on the Law of the Sea')
* the international trade in endangered animals and plants ('Convention on International Trade in Endangered Species of Wild Fauna and Flora')
* ships' dumping of harmful substances into the ocean ('International Convention for the Prevention of Pollution from Ships')
* the emission of dangerous substances into the air ('Convention on Long-Range Transboundary Air Pollution').

This is only a partial listing.

The UN Conference on Environment and Development (UNCED) to be held in Brazil in 1992 will probably decide to make further international agreements – on the climate, forests, species protection, and so on.

Yet none of these international treaties have brought far-reaching improvements in global environmental protection. We are currently experiencing a national and international discrepancy between environmental rhetoric and environmental policy. Almost without exception, politicians have added the terms 'ecology' and 'environmentally sound' to their standard repertoires; but little remains beyond the political rhetoric. Discussions at conferences and meetings rarely lead to concrete political action.

This lack of progress was clearly seen in the series of conferences on global warming. Two meetings in 1987, in Villach, Austria and Bellagio, Italy, concluded that maintaining current levels of CO_2 emissions will considerably increase global temperatures by the first half of the next century. The 1988 World Climate Conference in Toronto recommended a global reduction in CO_2 emissions of 20 per cent by the year 2005 and of 50 per cent by 2050.

The 'Statement of Policy Options to Curb Climatic Change' issued by international environmental groups in May 1989 made it clear that these recommendations do not go far enough. The environmentalists proposed – along with numerous other measures – a global reduction in CO_2 emissions of at least 20 per cent by the year 2000 and 50 per cent by 2015. In November 1989, at another conference in Nordwijk, Holland, environmental ministers from more than 60 countries again failed to make specific or binding resolutions concerning reduction goals. The next stations in this meeting marathon, the 1990 conferences in Bergen, Norway, Washington, and Geneva similarly brought no constructive action.

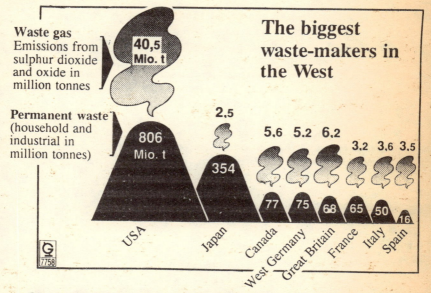

Waste gas Emissions from sulphur dioxide and oxide in million tonnes

Permanent waste (household and industrial in million tonnes)

The biggest waste-makers in the West

40,5 Mio. t

806 Mio. t — USA

2.5 — 354 — Japan

5,6 — 77 — Canada

5.2 — 75 — West Germany

6.2 — 68 — Great Britain

3.2 — 65 — France

3,6 — 50 — Italy

3.5 — 16 — Spain

G 7758

Once again the inertia came from the United States, Great Britain, the Soviet Union and Japan. They consider their economic performance capabilities endangered by CO_2 reductions and demand further scientific evidence for the relationship between CO_2 emissions and atmospheric warming.

The 'non-resolutions' of Nordwijk and Bergen show the bankruptcy of international environmental policy-making. They confirm again that the lack of binding agreements is not primarily the fault of the developing countries, but rather that of the industrial states. The dominance of economic interests and the sluggishness of the international negotiation process have prevented responsible action today for environmentally sound development in the future. The few progressive industrial states that place great value on solving global environmental problems – like Norway, Sweden, the Netherlands or Denmark – are among the 'dwarfs' of international politics. Their negotiating power is unfortunately not strong enough to achieve a breakthrough.

Further negotiations over the contents of an international climate agreement took place during 1991. The goal was to have specific protocols to present at the UNCED conference in Brazil in 1992. However, the hopes for making climate protection an urgent international priority have sunk because the Gulf War and its tremendous costs will mean less funding is available for critical ecological renewal.

European Community environmental policy

The European Community is an increasingly important level for West German environmental policy-making. The EC now sets the timing and framework of its member states' environmental policies. With the ratification on 1 July 1987 of the Single European Act, environmental protection was for the first time expressly recognized and incorporated in treaties as a political goal (Article 130 r-t).

Even though ecology is explicitly mentioned as a priority, environmental policy-making remains secondary to policies aimed at pushing 'European market integration'. The EC, in other words, will not allow an independent environmental policy that matches the importance of economic policies. In the face of growth and integration-oriented transportation, energy, agricultural and industrial policies, environmental standards will slip out of view and pollution will increase, not decrease.

The industrial states' one-sided preference for technocratic 'repair concepts' and their refusal to place the environmentally extremely harmful production and consumption model of the 'First World' up for public debate, determine the concrete form of international treaties and contracts. The industrial development model sets the conditions under which international environmental policy-making must be carried out.

Defining conditions and structural ecology

We demand that all international treaty-making on the future use of resources and emissions be publicly discussed and approved. The same applies to multinational institutions and programmes dedicated to the protection of inter-regional ecosystems (for example, tropical forests, Antarctica) and for all those financial organizations substantially involved in money transfers from North to South and West to East (the EC, multilateral development banks, IMF, and such organizations as GATT). Too much 'environmental policy' is hidden from the public view, and secrecy in such matters almost inevitably means 'appeasing' the public rather than dealing with the issues.

Only a radical rejection of 'catch-up industrialization' – of world market orientation at any price, of the chemicalization of all areas of life, of high energy consumption and 'cars for all' – will substantially improve the global environment.

With current global environmental problems threatening much of humanity's existence, it is clear that preserving our natural environment should be fundamental to shaping global economic relations. International organizations and governments have agreed upon the concept detailed in the Brundtland Report, that of 'long-term development'. However, this concept also follows the current development paradigms of industrial society, calling for ecological modernization that combines international economic growth with environmentally sound technology. Thus a five- to ten-fold increase in global industrial production within just a few decades is expected and supported.

But after-the-fact strategies that try to repair harmful production methods and environmental damage that should be prevented in the first place are not enough to counter the coming global environmental crisis. The 'industrialization of environmental protection' through growth in environmental protection technology cannot help us reach the goal of an ecological world economy based on solidarity. Such an economy must be oriented towards efficient ways to meet the basic needs of the poor and destitute. These must be accompanied by changes in the production and consumption standards of the wealthy North and of Southern elites. The satisfaction of basic needs worldwide on a socially and ecologically sustainable basis is central to our alternative development strategy.

Unlike ecological modernization, structural ecology starts with production, trade and consumption patterns and asks how ecological balance can be reached by changing these structures. The results will be measured by how close they come to reaching the goal of global ecological balance.

Structural ecology would replace environmentally dangerous production and consumption with ecologically sound forms, and is therefore the crucial complement to ecological modernization through environmentally sound technology. Ecological structural changes offer the sensible handling and reuse and recycling of resources as an alternative to further unlimited exploitation of ecosystems and finite resources. The goal is to reduce emissions of harmful substances from production and consumption to the point of eliminating their widespread circulation in the atmosphere.

Immediate actions

The far-reaching changes needed in the industrial countries and in the Third World point the way to a lasting and environmentally sound development. This development is conceivable by combining environmental modernization (the use of environmentally sound technology worldwide) and structural ecology – replacing environmentally destructive production and consumption patterns with ecologically sound models. Examples are energy-saving forms of production and consumption and the use of more environmentally sound and renewable energy sources worldwide.

The industrial states must take the lead in radical ecological restructuring of the global economy. Only when they have ecological credibility can they persuade countries of the Third World to abandon the socially and environmentally destructive course of 'catch-up industrialization'.

Due to the differences in the kinds of problems, their causes and the existing capacities for solving them, different long-range concepts for new West-West (EC, OECD), West-East and North-South environmental policies must be developed, based on the previously described principles. Above all, internal OECD environmental policies must try to set an international example. Energy consumption and associated emissions must be drastically reduced. The transportation sector must be environmentally restructured. Production of environmentally dangerous substances – especially industrial chemicals – must be discontinued. The flood of waste must be stopped. Agricultural practices must be ecologically restructured and large-scale reforestation initiated.

Some of the specific methods used to reach this goal have been outlined in our *Umbauprogramm* ('Reconstruction Programme'). Chapter 4 details proposals for bans on certain imports and exports, and the establishment of a World Economic Council to co-ordinate needed economic and environmental policies. Demands for the democratization and decentralization of industry and commerce will be explained in Chapter 7.

Debt cancellation: The Green Party supports a radical break from past and present 'development' paradigms. A reordering of global economic conditions is necessary to give Third World countries a fair chance of finding their own way, one that both satisfies people's basic needs and protects the natural environment.

As explained in Chapters 4 and 7, a basic prerequisite for this is comprehensive international debt cancellation. The ever-increasing debt burden and forced foreign currency acquisition for interest and repayment obligations increase the pressure to exploit resources and overuse ecosystems. The five countries – Brazil, Peru, Columbia, Zaire and Indonesia – that together have 60 per cent of the remaining tropical forests are among the largest debtor nations. Debt cancellation is an important prerequisite for preservation of their natural resources.

Arms conversion: The Worldwatch Institute in Washington, DC has calculated that it would cost approximately $770 trillion to halt the worldwide trend of environmental destruction by the turn of the century. This sum is approximately equal to annual global military expenditures. Disarmament thus offers a chance to finance the necessary expenditures for the preservation of the planet's natural environment.

An International Fund for the Environment: To begin a comprehensive programme for damage-reduction and structural ecology in the Third World, an International Fund for the Environment should be established, and should benefit the developing countries above all, but should also include the former Comecon countries. The Fund for the Environment is a central component of a climate convention for which we will present detailed proposals below.

The Fund for the Environment should be financed by an international tax on primary and atomic energy. This tax should vary according to the specific CO_2 emissions of the different primary energy sources, without creating advantages for the use of atomic energy. The accumulated emissions of CFCs should also be considered for similar taxes. The lion's share of the Fund's financing must come from the industrial states. We think that each country's contribution should be set at approximately one per cent of gross national product.

Cost of Military spending and social or ecological measures compared

Armaments	Cost ($)	Social/Ecological
Trident II submarine & F18 jet fighters	100bn	Estimated costs for cleaning up the 10,000 most dangerous special garbage dumps in the US
Stealth-bomber	68bn	Two-thirds of estimated costs of carrying out pescribed waste purificationin the US until year 2000
SDI budgets for fiscal year 1988-1992	38bn	Removal of high radioactive waste in the US
Worldwide armaments production for 2 weeks	30bn	Yearly costs of the planned UN decade of water and sewage
W. German expenditure on military procurements, research & developments in 1985	10.75bn	Estimated cost of cleaning up German sector of the North Sea
Worldwide 3-day moratorium on arms production	6.5 bn	5-year programme for saving the tropical rainforests
Development of Midget-man intercontinental missile	6bn	Yearly cost for reduction of SO_2 emissions in the US of around 8-12 m. tons p.a.
worldwide 2-day moratorium on arms production	4.8bn	Yearly costs of the UN programme to prevent desertification in the Thrid world for 20 yrs
US production of atomic warheads for 6 months, fiscal year 1987	4bn	US energy saving measures, fiscal years 1980-87
SDI research, fiscal year 1987	3.7bn	Means of building a solar powerworks for a town of 200000 inhabitants
Weapons production in EC for 10 days	2bn	Yearly cost for cleaning up special waste dumps in 10 EC countries until year 2000
1 Trident submarine	1.4bn	5-year programme for innoculation against deadly diseases that would prevent 1m deaths every year
3 B-1B bombers	680m	State production of renewable energy in the US, fiscal years 1983-85
Armaments production in Ethiopia for 2 months	50m	Yearly cost of UN programme to fight desertification in Ethiopia
1 atomic bomb test	12m	Installation of 80 000 handpumps in the Third World
Operational cost of a B-1B bomber for 1hr	21 000	Cost of medical treatment of mothers and children in 10 African villages whereby IMR can be reduced by half

source: Worldwide Institute, various sources from the World Watch Report, 'The State of the World 1989-90', Fischer Verlag, Frankfurt.

The Green Party further suggests that over the next decade developing countries' payments into this Fund should be calculated but not levied. The former Comecon states, whose economies are in the midst of massive restructuring, should also be exempt from making payments, under certain conditions, for a few years.

The Fund for the Environment should be established within the structures of the United Nations. There must, however, be a guarantee of more openness than there is today. To make that possible, environmental groups and primarily the people affected must be a strong presence in the start-up and allocation process of such a fund.

A tropical forest agreement: The Green Party is working hard to see that the protection of tropical forests progresses with utmost urgency at national and international levels. Tropical forests are the richest and most complex ecosystems on earth. They are critical for the natural global balance and climate stability, regionally and globally. The industrial countries share responsibility for the destruction of tropical forests. But they also have a direct interest in preserving these interregional ecosystems.

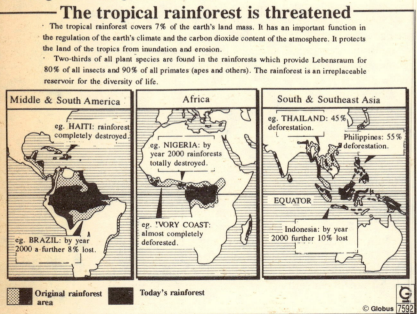

The tropical rainforest is threatened

· The tropical rainforest covers 7% of the earth's land mass. It has an important function in the regulation of the earth's climate and the carbon dioxide content of the atmosphere. It protects the land of the tropics from inundation and erosion.

· Two-thirds of all plant species are found in the rainforests which provide Lebensraum for 80% of all insects and 90% of all primates (apes and others). The rainforest is an irreplaceable reservoir for the diversity of life.

| Middle & South America | Africa | South & Southeast Asia |

eg. HAITI: rainforest completely destroyed.

eg. NIGERIA: by year 2000 rainforests totally destroyed.

eg. THAILAND: 45% deforestation.

Philippines: 55% deforestation.

EQUATOR

eg. IVORY COAST: almost completely deforested.

Indonesia: by year 2000 further 10% lost.

eg. BRAZIL: by year 2000 a further 8% lost.

Original rainforest area   Today's rainforest

© Globus 7592

The implementation of effective protective strategies must not create economic or other disadvantages in Third World countries. We must see the required expenditures for tropical forest protection as part of the ecological burden-sharing between North and South. The Green Party therefore calls for the conclusion of an international agreement for the protection of tropical forests, with five concrete goals:

1. protection of the still remaining primary forests from all human interference, with the exception of traditional and ecologically sound uses;
2. lasting protection of the living space and environment of all indigenous forest populations through the guarantee of inalienable property rights and cultural identity;
3. conversion of destructive farming methods to environmentally sound ones;
4. reforestation in destroyed or degraded areas following socially and naturally compatible criteria;
5. improvement of agricultural use outside tropical forests, so as to secure the population's food and firewood supplies.

This Tropical Forest Agreement should be financially supported by a tropical forest sub-fund under the Fund for the Environment. Under present conditions countries with tropical forests can only abstain from using these lands if they receive compensatory payments allowing them simultaneously to restructure their production and agricultural methods.

Outline for a climate agreement: Forest and climate protection must be bound together in such a way that no one-sided demands are placed on the Third World and, at the same time, that the industrial countries are compelled to restructure their societies. In this way the battle against the ozone hole and the greenhouse effect will become the central goal of international environmental policy. However, organizing a climate agreement raises some basic questions.

* Which climate-relevant gases must be reduced and by how much?
* In what areas should we place our initial emphasis?
* Who should carry the main responsibility for emission reductions?
* With what means should the necessary reductions be achieved?

Focus on CFCs and CO_2: Basically all greenhouse gases – CFCs, CO_2, methane, surface ozone and nitrous oxide – must be reduced as much as possible. Realistic analysis of the problem shows, however, that some gases can be limited more quickly than others. Our attention in the next years must focus on CFCs and CO_2, as these substances together account for some two-thirds of the greenhouse effect (CO_2 for 50 per cent, CFCs for 17 per cent). Furthermore, CFCs are almost solely responsible for the destruction of the ozone layer.

Worldwide use of CFCs must cease completely within the next five years. More than 90 per cent of CFCs are produced in the industrial states, but are not crucial to industrial production. A complete halt in their production will involve only minor structural problems. The Montreal Protocol, as revised in June 1990, calls for a binding international cessation of production of CFCs by the year 2000. But this is inadequate; given the urgency of the situation, this deadline is too late. Another problem is that the Protocol does not control or ban substitute chemicals such as the partially halogenated CFCs. What is needed are alternatives to CFCs without chemicals. Instead, industry and business are moving towards alternative chemicals. Environmentally sound substitute technologies and processes must be made available to the developing countries, some of which are only now beginning to produce CFCs.

The situation with CO_2 is less clear. Carbon dioxide emissions directly reflect the size and structure of a country's energy, industry and transportation sectors. A well-known German climatologist maintains that limiting global warming to an increase of one to two degrees celsius, which is considered tolerable, will require the following CO_2 reductions:

* by 2000 a reduction of at least 37 per cent of 1980 levels;
* by 2020 a reduction of at least 71 per cent of 1980 levels;
* by 2050 a reduction of at least 90 per cent of 1980 levels.

Achieving these or even more moderate goals will require radical energy conservation in the industrial states and the establishment of 'climate-sound' development in Third World countries. The Western OECD states can achieve such development if energy prices are increased and energy efficiency is taken seriously. We have demonstrated that one necessary prerequisite for this is a more decentralized energy supply. At the moment it seems impossible for the former Comecon states and developing countries to achieve less-dependent paths of development on their own. Help must be forthcoming from the Western OECD states.

Measures to reduce carbon dioxide emissions – improving energy efficiency in power plants and motor vehicles, developing renewable energy sources, increasing use of building insulation and reducing individual private transportation – all contribute to limiting greenhouse gases. The less fossil fuels are used, the less CO_2 surface ozone, methane, and nitrous oxide are produced.

In our opinion, a global climate agreement in the foreseeable future must include three main elements:

* far-reaching voluntary commitments to restraint by wealthy nations;
* the establishment of a world climate fund (within the Fund for the Environment) to benefit, first and foremost, developing countries and the former Comecon states;
* comprehensive public participation in measures taken to protect the climate by recipient countries.

The following steps are necessary:

* The CFC-producing nations must halt CFC production by 1995 within the guidelines of the Montreal Protocol. Governments will be called upon to issue immediate and comprehensive bans on CFC use where it can be eliminated today without problems.
* The OECD states must take the lead in the area of CO_2 reduction and commit themselves to reduce CO_2 emissions by 30 per cent by the year 2000 and 60 per cent by 2010.

* A climate convention should be adopted under the control of the United Nations Environmental Programme (UNEP) by 1992. At the same time, protocols for the reduction of specific greenhouse gases, similar to the Montreal Protocol regulating CFCs, must be passed, especially for CO_2 and methane. Time schedules and quotas for each country must be established in these protocols. In the case of violations, it must be possible for the international community to invoke sanctions.

* The establishment of a climate fund within the Fund for the Environment should be central to the climate convention. It seems reasonable to group the areas of potential funding into at least three categories:

1) introduction of CFC-free technologies and production methods in the developing countries;

2) assistance for means of reducing CO_2, especially in the areas of energy and transportation;

3) preservation of tropical forests and assistance in reforestation and soil protection programmes.

Restructuring international organizations

An appropriate institutional framework must be found to guide worldwide ecological and social developments, the passage and improvement of international agreements and treaties and the implementation of concrete protection programmes – preservation of tropical forests, protection of Antarctica, containing desertification. National and bilateral policies are not strong enough to deal with environmental crises, and climate change cannot be solved by such treaties alone. Instead the emphasis must be placed on multilateral approaches. Democratically legitimated supervisory authorities must be given the power to issue sanctions when necessary, and organizations must be provided with the appropriate expertise to implement environmental policies.

At present international environmental policies and environmental law have been established within so many different international and regional organizations that it is difficult to maintain an overview of their functioning. In the past, international environmental policies have also broken down over the principle of sovereignty that forbids interference in a nation's exploitation of its natural resources.

An international environmental law is thus needed that can set boundaries for national behaviour when necessary. The basis for such international law can be the United Nations World Charter for Nature, the environmental programme prepared by the United Nations Environmental Programme (UNEP) and adopted by the UN General Assembly in 1982. This Charter is the first comprehensive international document to call for the moderate and responsible handling of natural resources and that regulates the safeguarding of ecosystems.

So far, however, this World Charter has had at best a consciousness-raising function. In the future, legally binding responsibilities of states and corporations must be stipulated, as is the case with the Human Rights Charter (see Chapter 3). An international environmental agreement could then mandate ecological as well as social criteria in international law for the activities of all UN organizations. Furthering this goal should also be one key task of the UN Council on World Economics whose formation we propose in this book.

Multilateral development banks

Multilateral development banks and the International Monetary Fund currently play important roles in the world economy and in development financing. They carry considerable responsibility when it comes to the exploitation and overuse – or protection – of natural resources. For this reason the World Bank has prepared itself organizationally and conceptually for a possible role as a co-ordination centre for environmental protection activities in the Third World.

Although it is known for its environmentally disastrous policies, the World Bank is being supported by the West in the framework of a Climate Convention to administer and distribute climate funding. The dependence of many Third World countries on one single organization that organizes North-South financing will inevitably increase if the World Bank is given this additional role.

To the extent that World Bank credit policies contribute to ecological industrial restructuring in the Third World and work towards conversion to more efficient energy strategies, they deserve support. But it is important that the World Bank, the IMF and multilateral development banks ensure that their overall economic strategies and adjustment programmes are environmentally sound.

The IMF and the World Bank will not have environmental credibility as long as their policies remain narrowly oriented towards increased exports, improved short-term ability to make payments, and short-term profits that ignore the social and ecological costs of investment decisions in their cost-benefit analyses.

Expanding the World Bank's monopoly prevents or delays efforts towards democratizing international organizations. The distribution of voting rights in the World Bank favours the industrial states, therefore they define the actions and protective measures that will limit the roles of national governments and especially of non-governmental organizations. (This problem is discussed further in Chapter 4.)

The UN Environmental Programme (UNEP)

We support the financial and organizational strengthening of UNEP, which is currently one of the weakest organizations in the UN family due to insufficient funds and a lack of authority. UNEP could be strengthened through allocation of resources from the Fund for the Environment and structural reform. One necessary reform is that other UN organizations (especially the UNDP and FAO) and the World Bank, whose policies have far-reaching effects for the ecological aspect of the development process, should either transfer authority to UNEP or be ready to co-ordinate and co-operate closely.

The UNEP must also speed up its conceptual work. Strategies applying to individual countries should be drawn up in close co-operation with each responsible UN economic commission and local and regional non-governmental organizations. Starting points for further conceptual development of UNEP policies are offered by the extensive data compiled over recent years from UNEP co-ordination of specific protection programmes such as that for the Mediterranean, the global environmental observation systems GEMS and INFOTERRA, and the register of potentially dangerous chemicals.

Increased financial support and expanded authority must be combined with comprehensive voting and participation rights for international environmental and non-governmental organizations in conceptualizing future development and environmental strategies. UNEP must be strengthened in conjunction with the reorientation and reorganization of the UN that is addressed in Chapter

7. There is also a need to strengthen local authority. The global environmental crisis is made up of many local crises. Directly affected social groups almost everywhere fight to preserve local ecosystems and natural resources for social, economic or political reasons. Resistance to socially and environmentally destructive modernization strategies has led people to trace supposedly local environmental problems back to their international, economic and political sources. In many cases, the local population knows best how to protect the threatened ecosystem.

Thus 500,000 Brazilian rubber-tree tappers from the Amazonian lowlands whose existence depends on the preservation of the tropical rain forest called attention to the global consequences of tropical forest destruction. The affected forest populations in India, Malaysia, the Philippines and Brazil protest against the destruction of their environment by invading international lumber companies and white settlers. They have resorted to actions that have met with state and privately organized repression directed especially against environmental activists; these activists receive support from international environmental and consumer movements.

Environmental education

The preparatory work for an international climate agreement is currently being done by an intergovernmental committee, the Intergovernmental Panel for Climate Change (IPCC). At present the industrialized states are mainly involved in the negotiation process, although a few non-governmental organizations and representatives from Third World countries are gradually being included. Societal pressure from below and from Third World countries will be decisive to achieve extensive emission reduction goals and for the democratic organizing of existing or to-be-established institutions responsible for the management of the Environmental Fund.

The task of the Green Party must thus be to further the discussion on what measures are necessary to prevent climate change, to point out the differing interests in our society and to help build opposition to powerful economic lobbies (like those for energy and motor vehicles).

The climate catastrophe is a central challenge to us all. But catastrophic scenarios just lead to feelings of hopelessness and political impotence. Instead we must help break through this powerlessness with appropriate consciousness-raising campaigns and through working in coalition with emancipatory movements North and South, East and West.

The prerequisite for strengthening local activists is returning knowledge and authority to the public, through environmental education and decentralized decision-making structures. We also need to reverse the progressive alienation between human beings and nature. Through greater consciousness, education and participation we can combine our personal attitudes and lifestyles with an awareness of existing global and international problems finally to achieve a global awareness of responsibility.

3. Restructuring international trade in commodities and services

Globalization and privatization of the world economy

International trade in the areas of commodities, patents and services has become globalized. The damaging ecological effects of our Western industrial model are exported with increasing intensity to poor nations which, in their desperate economic circumstances, grasp at any straw. An example of this is the export of toxic waste to Third World countries which are unable safely to dispose of these substances.

Today transnational corporations predominate in the capitalist world market, operating beyond national borders and restrictions. These global enterprises, almost without exception controlled by Western capital, increasingly lose their connection to their country of origin. Politicians pushing for the free trade paradigm support this trend even though globalization undermines and dismantles their own parliamentary power. In addition, those sectors of the world economy which are so far largely unregulated expand rapidly through technological innovation in the areas of information, communication, transportation and gene technology.

In the process of increasing internationalization and deregulation, the relationship between politics and economics is being fundamentally redefined on a global scale. Opposing tendencies of economic integration and political fragmentation have caused a new kind of privatization of the world economy. This allows transnational corporations to continue pushing their power politics and profit-oriented interests. For, according to the free trade paradigm, in the end there should be no barriers at all to global capital exploitation. More than 75 per cent of international trade in commodities and services takes place among highly industrialized Western economies. The fact that more than one-third of world trade is carried out internally between corporations also reflects the powerful position of transnational enterprises.

The Eastern European and Third World states can do little other than accept the capitalistic world market as the framework and condition for their foreign economic integration. Some countries, especially in South-east Asia, have achieved a competitive status in certain markets for consumer and capital goods and have even caused difficulties for traditional branches of industry in Western countries. But increasingly the overwhelming majority of Third World economies are being forced out of the world market. As their relative technological backwardness grows, their competitiveness in international markets declines. Although the quantity of their exports often rises, their share of total world trade as expressed in dollars declines.

International exchange relations (terms of trade) for commodities and services are marked by an increasing disparity. Prices for export products from poor economies, especially for natural resources and simple industrial goods, are reaching rock bottom while prices for high-technology goods from the industrialized countries rise. The extreme dependency of the poorer states on foreign knowledge and know-how is apparent in the one-sided orientation of the international patent and licensing business.

Ironically, the emphasis on production for export to gain foreign exchange for debt servicing speeds the decline in prices for debtor nations' commodities. The additional supply of Third World goods is not met with more demand in the West. Thus prices fall. Cuts in wages become 'necessary' to reduce costs of production and this leads to reductions in workers' and human rights as well as lower environmental standards. In the free production zones of low-wage countries, foreign firms hire women and children to work for the world market under exploitative conditions. The World Bank and the International Monetary Fund (IMF) are responsible for adjustment programmes which escalate this downward price spiral, particularly in the natural resource market where price hikes are urgently needed to promote energy savings.

Germany has become a major power in the world economic system. In 1989 West Germany was the second largest exporter after Japan (641 billion DM), and had the highest surplus in international commodity trading (135 billion DM). The colossal positive balance in the current account that year (104 billion DM) allowed West Germany to become one of the most powerful creditors worldwide. Germany's economic prosperity and international influence is to a great extent based on this dominant world market position.

The type of goods and services traded and directions of trade relations are determined by the global distribution of power, not peoples' needs. Global trade structures are thus oriented towards the wealthy nations and rich minorities in poor nations. Because two-thirds of humankind do not have cash incomes worth mentioning, the currents of world trade pass them by. This state of affairs makes it ever more urgent to discuss thoroughly a restructuring of world trade on the basis of ethical values. An ecological world economy based on solidarity has as its goal a different distribution of wealth and income on a global scale. Far-reaching changes in the scope, make-up and orientation of global goods and services exchange will result.

Under the high social and ecological standards in international trade which we propose in this programme, poorer countries would experience massive reductions in sales because important competitive advantages would be removed.

We therefore also emphasize compensation in the form of debt cancellation, increased transfer payments and guaranteed market access at cost-covering prices. The financial resources necessary for this should be provided by the wealthy nations.

Our ideas for change in world trade are linked to the present system of international agreements, policy instruments, and institutions; but these must be qualitatively transformed. Responsibilities must be defined, the internal distribution of power reformed, and participation of social movements guaranteed.

Today there is a great variety of international institutions each concerned with specific aspects of world trade, but these institutions are working under certain political constraints. Overall problems in the existing structures include the possibilities for national non-compliance and insufficient international power to impose sanctions, as well as the hegemony of governments and transnational enterprises.

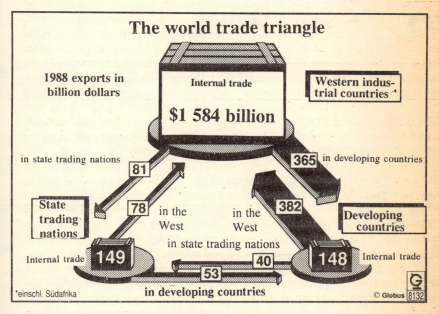

The world trade triangle

1988 exports in billion dollars

Internal trade

$1 584 billion

Western industrial countries *

in state trading nations 81 365 in developing countries

State trading nations

78 in the West in the West 382 Developing countries

in state trading nations

Internal trade 149 40 148 Internal trade

53

in developing countries

*einschl. Südafrika © Globus 8132

Linking trade policy with human rights

World trade mechanisms relate directly to human rights. Through many United Nations agreements – including the conventions on civil and political as well as economic, social and cultural rights, the rulings of the International Labour Organization (ILO), and in regional human rights agreements – a highly differentiated system of human rights has been developed. Its different dimensions are considered to be equal in value and inseparable – political and social rights, women's rights, children's rights, protection against ethnic discrimination, and workers' rights. The 1986 declaration of the UN General Assembly on the right to development made demands on the world economic system in the interests of the poor populations.

Even to the extent that these standards have an internationally binding character, however, they are frequently blocked by the predominant economic and political interests, or neglected because independent bodies are unable to impose sanctions in case of violations. What is needed when it comes to human rights and other green/alternative priorities is for nations to agree to a limited and well-defined relinquishing of their powers of sovereignty on the basis of equality. For us, it is obvious that the globally active, economically powerful industrialized nations must take the lead in this process of self-restraint so that the poor nations, whose sovereignty is in fact considerably limited by external constraints, will be encouraged to take the same steps. Supranational organizations should have expanded authority, but on the premise that democratic controls on accountability and openness are guaranteed.

The contractual anchoring of human rights stipulations can be realized within the framework of the General Agreement on Trade and Tariffs (GATT). In October 1988 the European Parliament called on GATT member states to commit themselves to implementing basic ILO conventions on social protection rights in the service sector. The European Parliament proposed the creation of an advisory committee of the GATT and ILO, which would be commissioned to monitor fulfilment of the social stipulations and to recommend measures for effective application of the stipulations and for sanctions against the countries or enterprises which violate them. With a similar construction, the commitment of all sectors of international trade to such stipulations could be expanded to the complete catalogue of codified UN human rights.

The monitoring of human rights must not be restricted to the promotion, production and transport of individual goods, but must apply to the entire social system. Governments, international organizations and business enterprises as well as individuals must be held legally accountable for complaints or violations. With their membership of GATT, all participating governments and corporations would subject themselves to the decisions of an independent human rights' body, for example the International Court of Justice or a new Court for Human Rights. In the case of proven systematic violation they must expect a graded system of penalties and sanctions, such as bans on exports of products complained about, trade restrictions for specific groups of commodities, full boycotts, financial penalties and imprisonment for individuals.

Human rights' organizations and other social forces must have full access to such legal institutions. At present only governments can bring complaints to the International Court of Justice and proceedings in the Court can be taken only against a state when it specifically agrees. Before human rights' standards can be set in world trade all member states must agree fully to accept the Court's jurisdiction and its decision-making authority.

Currently, products on the world market cannot be monitored for the human rights or ecological conditions under which they are developed, produced, promoted and transported. The Green Party has therefore suggested an 'eco-clause' for GATT, to be monitored by an independent legal body such as a chamber of the International Court of Justice.

As with human rights, the violation of internationally binding ecological standards must be discouraged by effective sanctions. The procedures and also the limitations of this approach are similar to those for human rights' stipulations. The central component of the eco-clause should be a complete ban on international trade in products that contribute to the destruction of valuable natural areas and ecosystems. An example of this is pig-iron and steel-making in the east Amazon (Carajas), where primeval tropical forests are used to produce wood charcoal for smelting.

The world's remaining extensive natural systems – Antarctica, the ocean floor and primeval forests – should be protected from all destructive uses. Located outside national borders, they are the 'inheritance of humankind' and should serve the ecological interests of the international community.

The ecological regulations in GATT should build on the existing system of 'black lists', that have been developed by such UN organizations as the World Health Organization, the International Labour Organization and the Food and Agriculture Organization. (Even the GATT recently established a corresponding group.) The world market products listed are banned or restricted in the exporting country. They are mostly health endangering chemical or pharmaceutical substances (for example, pesticides and industrial chemicals) and consumer goods (certain cosmetic products and food additives). The international information network should protect peoples and the environment in the import countries from injury. The UN's third list is currently being compiled and contains 600 products whose use is either banned or restricted by 93 governments. Except for the Basel Convention on Toxic Waste, the system suffers from the fact that international authorities can only issue recommendations that are not legally binding. We therefore call for the lists to be compiled in a more complete and systematic manner than in the past. In the short-term the present codices must be strengthened, for example the FAO's code of conduct on the introduction and use of pesticides and insecticides.

The ecological costs and damage resulting from long-distance transportation of goods and people must be drastically reduced. This means quantitative reductions of volume transported. Economic costs of transport must be calculated with consideration given to depletion of non-renewable fuels, and environmental destruction. The framework of international conventions must make those who are responsible for these environmental costs pay for them.

International tourism in its current form must be reduced to avoid further environmental damage and destruction of host countries' cultural identities. Governments and international travel organizations should follow an internationally binding code of minimum standards. These would ensure the interests of people in the areas involved and prevent exploitative forms of travel, such as 'sex tourism'.

Social justice on a world scale

Political regulations must make it possible for economically weaker countries to trade on the world market in such a way that the basic needs of people in all societies are satisfied. Weaker states should be allowed to take protective measures unilaterally, or erect market barriers, waiving the principle of reciprocity in certain areas.

The privileges of the poorer states need to be considerably expanded by a global preference system graded according to the trading partners' economic diversity and strength. Bilateral relations and trade agreements may sometimes be the best way to improve the position of the weaker states in comparison with multilateral minimum standards. The central GATT principles of most-favoured nation status and non-discrimination should not be valid in trade between unequal partners. Nevertheless, the effectiveness of political trade concessions must not be over-estimated, because they cannot break down prevailing power structures either internationally or within individual societies. Safeguarding trade advantages has the hidden danger that failed economic strategies and dependencies will be maintained and that governments or national elites will profit, not the producers themselves.

We think that political action in the area of trade can help prevent further world market losses for the poorer countries. Taking a longer perspective however, we are working through a national restructuring policy programme, because a structural transformation of world trade must begin and be grounded in reforms in the highly industrialized societies. Far-reaching structural adjustments through social and ecological restructuring in the wealthy countries as well as breaking up international power structures – transnational concerns, power differences between governments – are necessary prerequisites for a new world trade order.

Concrete steps towards this goal are possible with the economic and political strengthening of the weaker states within the framework of South-South co-operation and regional economic communities. The Green Party supports the organizations that represent these interests, such as the Group of 77 within the UN, the Non-Aligned Movement and the South Commission, although we do not agree with every position. In April 1988 the Group of 77 formulated a trade preference system that we think deserves financial support from the wealthy states.

A crucial aspect of the Green Party concept of international economic policies is a simultaneous strengthening of social movements in poorer nations so that changes in world trade will result in real improvements for impoverished millions. But fundamental protection of the interests of the poor can only come with global acceptance of a socially just and environmentally sound development model.

GATT: The Uruguay Round negotiations and alternatives

The goal of the current GATT negotiations (The Uruguay Round) that began in 1986 is the reordering of world trade in commodities and services – against the declared will of many Third World countries. The dominant Western states are strenuously trying to expand the free-trade dogma to sectors that were previously excluded (agriculture, services, investments and intellectual property such as patents). Their strategic goal is first and foremost the unlimited liberalization in areas of services where they have a competitive edge – banking, insurance, transport, media and culture.

We reject this planned global annexation of national markets by financially strong Western enterprises; and we are fundamentally opposed to the elimination of national regulations in the service sector. If the capital-oriented liberalization cannot be averted, we support the demands of many Third World nations for more freedom for workers who want to move to high-wage countries. There must be a balance between capital and labour mobility, though we clearly plead for capital mobility on a reduced scale. This seems to be the prerequisite for regional development.

In our opinion the GATT negotiations should accept the central importance of agriculture in poorer countries and allow one-sided protective rights. On ecological grounds the chemical and energy-intensive surplus agricultural production in the highly industrialized states must be ended. Consumer interests in healthy, non-processed food should be given appropriate consideration in reformulating GATT guidelines (see also Appendix 3 on world agricultural trade).

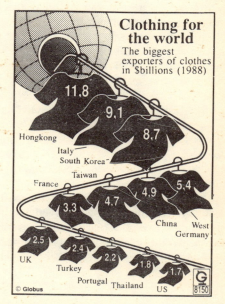

Clothing for the world
The biggest exporters of clothes in $billions (1988)

Hongkong 11,8
Italy 9,1
South Korea 8,7
Taiwan
France
China 3,3
4,7
4,9
West Germany 5,4
UK 2,5
Turkey 2,4
Portugal 2,2
Thailand 1,8
US 1,7
© Globus 8150

We reject the continued efforts of the dominating industrial nations within GATT to force extensive tariff reductions on Third World countries. Permanent 'tariff walls' make sense in many cases: they protect domestic manufacturers from competition with technologically superior and heavily capitalized foreign suppliers that can drive them out of the market. Tariffs also often provide an important means of financing investments in the infrastructures of poor nations. We also find GATT's fundamental rejection of barter trade unjustified. Especially in South-South, but also in East-West trade, direct exchange of goods offers possibilities for intensified economic relations unaffected by the ups and downs of the hard-currency based world market.

We oppose every attempt to increase international regulations over the protection of intellectual property – as in the current GATT negotiations and as favoured by the US. On the contrary, a system of compulsory licensing with a sliding scale of fees for poor countries should be established to increase access to protected knowledge and discoveries in areas basic to human needs – medicine, medical equipment, production methods, plant breeding. The two international conventions on copyrights, which contain exceptions for Third World countries, can serve as a model. When developing countries are unable to acquire a license on the commercial market to translate or reproduce books, they can apply to UNESCO for a compulsory one. But currently, this license is not granted for commercial reproduction or for export and applies only to literary, scientific or arts publications.

We are opposed to the ban on certain investment obligations within the limits of GATT (such as minimum domestic shares, exchange restrictions, equity capital) which are promoted by the United States in particular. The bans would completely eliminate any possibilities for conducting creative economy policy *vis à vis* foreign investors.

An example of a positive attempt to balance political interests in a sensitive industrial sector is the extension of the World Textiles Treaty within a new framework of workers' protection, social justice and ecological soundness. The working conditions in all participating states should be brought into line with the ILO's central standards, including working hours, minimum wage, social insurance, union rights and non-discrimination. And the economic interests of the poorest countries as suppliers must be given a well-co-ordinated special preference, with ecological aspects taken into consideration.

In our opinion GATT's status as an international treaty is inadequate. We are therefore working to see GATT develop into a regular sub-organization of the United Nations, one in which all countries can participate equally. In fact, after World War II the founding of such an 'International Trade Organization' was discussed. The charter for this new organization must authorize the full range of anti-trust and competition policy respecting the primacy of ecological and human rights and social principles. The interests of the populations of economically weaker countries should be supported for the long-term with one-sided rights. All interested non-governmental organizations must be guaranteed rights of access to and co-operation by world trade organizations.

Bans as an instrument of trade policy: Immediate effective intervention in the current world trade system is urgently needed to protect the environment and prevent war. The UN-organized trade embargo against Iraq is a case in point. Our goal is a complete halt to world trade in the following dangerous or environmentally or socially harmful products through strict bans on their export and import within the framework of GATT:

* trade in human organs;
* military goods and technology in the broadest sense;
* nuclear power plants and technology;
* tropical wood;
* products and living things produced with gene technology as well as the scientific processes used to create them;
* export of food products and livestock feed from famine areas;
* protected animals (endangered species) as well as products made from them (expanding on the Convention on International Trade in Endangered Species of Wild Fauna and Flora);
* environmentally destructive substances with high risk potential – such as ozone-destroying CFCs;
* hard drugs;
* toxic waste (the Convention on the Control of Transboundary Movements of Hazardous Wastes and their Disposal must be changed to include a complete trade ban).

The adjustment processes brought about by this should preferably be compensated by increased transfer payments.

The work of grassroots movements is crucial for accomplishing this extensive restructuring process. With public education and political campaigns, especially in the area of critical consumption, corresponding regulations at the national level could be enforced or speeded up.

Agreement on raw materials: Many developing economies are based on the export of one or several raw materials. This dependence is often a legacy of colonial control. Achieving fairer exchange conditions in world trade for these especially vulnerable countries requires special regulations to safeguard the prices of their irreplaceable raw materials. These include price increases and guaranteed sales quotas based on the degree of dependency and state of economic development.

On the one hand we support setting the price of raw materials in line with developments in the industrial goods sector (stabilizing of terms of trade through price indexing). On the other, it must be guaranteed that traditional production structures are not cast in stone – quite the opposite. Price supports should be used to encourage diversification to meet domestic or regional demand. The proceeds of price stability systems should benefit the direct producers as much as possible. Excessive production surpluses, for example the European 'milk lake' and 'butter mountain', can be prevented by establishing quantity limits for producing countries.

Previous agreements on raw materials have shown mixed results. A stabilization aimed exclusively at price guarantees would deplete the reserves of the compensation fund. In addition, price guarantees do not in any way ensure that producers will invest their receipts in their local economies to diversify their income sources for the future. But scepticism over the limited reach of previous attempts in this direction should not distract from real, if only partial, successes. Moreover, the costs of non-regulation are also considerable. After the collapse of the Coffee Agreement due to the suspension of quotas in the summer of 1989, coffee prices dropped 50 per cent. For many countries the attractiveness of the cultivatable alternative – drug crops – increased considerably, an outcome that will not improve international economic co-operation.

The Common Fund for Raw Materials of the UN Conference on Trade and Development (UNCTAD) started functioning in June 1989. It has two different and separately financed tasks. The first is funding buffer stocks of raw materials from the international Agreement on Raw Materials. The second involves financial support for new methods for production and marketing of raw materials. We recognize the limited room for negotiation within the framework of the previous structures of the Common Fund. But we conclude that further development is needed, emphasizing a completely restructured 'second window' in the direction of ecological production, fairer distribution and domestically oriented market diversification.

For example, organic agriculture could be specifically supported; this would also reduce the supply pressures. In certain cases a complete halt in raw materials extraction could be agreed upon for ecological reasons. The financial losses for the extracting industry could be compensated by long-term payments.

A new determination of the fund's function is only thinkable with a considerable increase in financial resources. Sales taxes in the wealthy countries on the products concerned, like coffee and tea, should be paid in full as contributions to the 'second window' we propose. We demand that EC funds for the STABEX and SYSMIN systems for the stabilization of raw materials proceeds likewise be transferred to the 'second window' without allowing a decline in the situation of the recipient countries.

Only a global agreement on raw materials can adequately account for the special needs of the countries dependent on them. Privileged special relationships with certain countries because of a colonial tradition should be rejected because they reinforce structures of dependency.

We suggest that the standards developed in this setting (for example the Lome Agreement) should become globally applicable. In view of the precarious situation of many raw materials countries, the speculative (destabilizing) interests in raw materials trading must be stopped, for instance by taxing contracts on the raw materials markets. The UN Conference on Trade and Development (UNCTAD), a multilateral institution that has traditionally represented the interests of the Third World, should be strengthened and its political value enhanced (see Appendix 2).

The consumer movement and alternative trade

The production and marketing processes of world market commodities must be reformed so as to expand the possibilities for conscientious consumers to negotiate. Choices between products based on ethical and ecological criteria can be made only if one has specific information on origin and trade conditions. We recognize the extreme importance of the critical consumer movement for the accomplishment of a new order in world trade. We want to help create suitable conditions for consumers' rights of information through comprehensive labelling requirements (for example for commodities produced with the use of child labour) and we support exemplary trade approaches such as 'transparent' or understandable marketing channels. However, the effectiveness of the critical consumer movement will be determined by market structures. Reducing the concentrated power of the supply side improves the effectiveness of boycotts and other forms of consumer pressure.

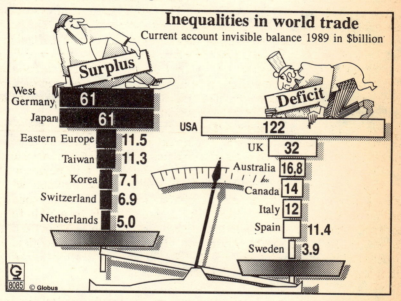

Inequalities in world trade
Current account invisible balance 1989 in $billion

Surplus

West Germany	61
Japan	61
Eastern Europe	11.5
Taiwan	11.3
Korea	7.1
Switzerland	6.9
Netherlands	5.0

Deficit

USA	122
UK	32
Australia	16.8
Canada	14
Italy	12
Spain	11.4
Sweden	3.9

8085 © Globus

Today, for many Third World products, especially luxury goods such as coffee, tea and cocoa, proven models exist in Western countries for a world trade based on solidarity. An example is the West German Society for the Support of Partnership with the Third World (GEPA), organized by church youth groups. Typically, products are purchased from co-operative businesses or from countries with basic needs-oriented policies under special market conditions – a higher price for the direct producer, support for social measures, or minimum price and long-term purchasing agreements. In the Netherlands, good quality coffee purchased under these conditions and processed in various roasting houses is available in all supermarkets under the brand 'Max Havelar'.

The Greens have themselves participated in and organized grassroots initiatives towards world trade. In our opinion, there is a considerable untapped demand in West Germany for world market goods that are produced under ecologically sound and socially fair conditions and bring fair prices to the manufacturers. We know that political changes at governmental and multilateral levels cannot be effective if they are not based on similarly oriented societal impulses.

Democratization of world trade

These proposed institutions and methods for restructuring world trade are doomed to failure if the real balance of power is not fundamentally changed between those involved – corporations, governments, social movements, individual consumers and farmers. The ethical values and interests that the Greens represent are based on a democracy that affects all existing structures. We are especially striving to remove or limit the power of leading investment groups and transnational corporations in world trade with commodities and services. The prerequisite for this is the establishment of globally binding minimum ecological and social standards for transnational corporations' trade or capital investment. Corporate break-ups and new forms of social property in the dominant capitalist countries contribute further to the realization of human rights, structural ecology and demilitarization (see Chapter 6).

The Greens see the strengthening of the opposition (unions, consumers, environmental organizations and so on) as crucial to removing the concentration of power from the hands of transnational corporations. The structures of all multilateral institutions must be reorganized in such a way that social forces are granted co-operation and voting rights. Within the ILO this is already becoming reality. The ILO's trilateral construction allows unions and business groups to work alongside governments. The position of the International Organization of Consumers Unions (IOCU), which currently has an advisory status within many UN organizations such as UNESCO, UNICEF and FAO, must also be enhanced. The relations between international regions of differing economic strengths within the international system must be redefined on an equal basis.

To limit the concentration of power in the world economy caused by ever greater creditor positions, the Greens support a move towards balanced foreign accounts. In this way the export of unemployment could also be prevented. When it comes to the trade balance in a narrow sense, however, wealthy countries must report surpluses and balance them out with appropriate transfer payments in the form of non-redeemable contributions. During discussions over the founding of the IMF in the 1940s, John Maynard Keynes developed an interesting solution for the international balancing of accounts, namely penalty interests on surpluses.

The UN's institutional structures must be strengthened in several different ways. We are calling for the establishment of a UN World Economic Council with decision-making authority. All other multilateral world economic institutions (IMF, GATT, the World Bank, UNCTAD, and so on) must subject themselves to the decisions of general principle of this highest committee (see Chapters 4 and 7).

Parallel to the creation of global structures, the level of regional and sub-regional co-operation and broader participation of social forces must be strengthened, in order to prevent unjustified centralization and bureaucratization. The current structure of the OECD must also be fundamentally questioned. As an organization that has served to co-ordinate and safeguard the interests of the highly industrialized countries, a part of the OECD's functions should be passed on to the UN World Economic Council. In the area of European co-operation, these functions should be assigned to the UN Economic Commission for Europe (ECE).

The legal organization of economic relations between nations (for example, investment protection treaties, treaties for the prevention of double taxing) should not occur at the bilateral level, but rather in a multilateral context with special consideration for poorer states' interests. The West German system of bilateral agreements in use worldwide as a way to cement competitive positions should therefore be abandoned. The newly created Multilateral Investment Guarantee Agency (MIGA) of the World Bank can only provide a framework for a fair balancing of interests between countries of origin and host countries if voting rights within the MIGA are reformed to benefit weaker host countries, and if global social and ecological minimum standards for foreign direct investment are put into effect.

West Germany faces a special economic adjustment problem in its balance of payments. In order to reduce the trade surpluses enough to bring the balance of payments to zero, all direct and indirect forms of export subsidies must be eliminated. This is especially a problem for the principle of tied aid applied in development programmes and the Hermes export insurance by which the West German government insures exports in high-risk areas. The Hermes yearly deficit of more than one billion DM is completely transferred to the federal budget. The system of foreign Chambers of Commerce financed with public funds is also a hidden subsidy of private foreign economic interests despite all the many free-trade declarations.

4. Restructuring the international financial system and reforming development relations

Why reorganize the international financial system?

A well-functioning international monetary system is a precondition for an ecological and socially just global economy. It is needed to manage international transfers of surpluses and deficits more adequately. An inadequate financial system is counter-productive. It reduces living standards, prevents development opportunities and encourages resource waste. The Greens advocate a stable monetary system that will put international financial policies on a democratically legitimated path.

International financial relations have been in a permanent state of crisis since the breakdown of the post-war Bretton Woods System in the early 1970s, when the United States' economic and political hegemony and its position as lender of last resort in the Western financial system began to falter. Since then there have been no new agreements to stabilize international financial relations. Today international monetary and financial policies are *ad hoc* decisions based mostly on chance or the principle euphemistically known as 'muddling through'. This has created a potentially explosive situation. There are only informal agreements about how to deal with financial accidents, and in many instances the poorest countries bear the burden. The debt crisis in the Third World provides a sad example of this.

International banks, multilateral financial institutions, central bankers and the finance ministers of the industrial countries seem content with the current system. It allows them maximum room to manoeuvre. The central bankers' strategy is based on a restrictive financial policy and the institutionalization of the principles of 'international monetarism' and the so-called policy of stability. The rise of real interest rates in the 1980s is one result of this strategy. The central bankers have succeeded in establishing their supremacy over other forms of economic intervention such as fiscal, labour, development and environmental policies.

At the same time, the central banks have achieved *de facto* freedom from democratic parliamentary control. The many disturbances in the international financial system, such as the disastrous debt crisis, stock market crashes and the chronic overvaluation of the dollar, are simply swept under the carpet and discussed in the most limited framework possible. Nothing is less desirable to the central banks than public control; any form of democratic participation makes them see red.

International bankers have said that reform is necessary. But their idea of reform is deregulation of financial transactions and more freedom from capital controls, nationally and internationally. They argue that open borders for international capital are necessary to maximize the financial system's efficiency and to best allocate economic resources. The bankers' sole concern, however, is increased business. Effects on the economy as a whole are of only secondary importance to them. Recently completed legal changes to create one single European (EC) financial market is a product of this thinking. It will be one of the least regulated financial markets in the world.

The fact that the post-war reconstruction of West Germany and Japan was only possible with targeted controls on interest and capital transactions, as well as stringent regulation is completely ignored. Nonetheless, the appeal of the ideology of financial *laissez-faire*, especially upon conservative politicians, is great. Our attempt to win acceptance for an alternative paradigm must work not only at the level of policy-making, but also at the level of economic theory.

Third World debt

In co-operation with the Third World solidarity movement, the Greens have dealt with issues of international finance in the context of the Third World debt crisis. The Green Party is critical of the 'case by case' examination of indebtedness sought by financial managers. There is no doubt that much of the debt was badly invested or used for consumption by ruling elites. Still the trigger of the debt crisis was pulled by the macro-economic policy-makers of industrial states. Their policies set the framework for Third World development potentials. An example is the monetary policy of the two largest creditor countries, Japan and West Germany, which was and remains aimed at increasing their export surpluses and thereby increasing import prices and thus, in effect, prevent Third World commodities from entering the market. With this set-up, developing countries have no real chance to establish footholds in industrial countries' markets. In other words, the debtor countries' attempt to pay their debts with money earned through exports fails, because industrial countries are wary of the competition and close their markets. In this way, the establishment of effective international mechanisms to settle the balance of payments deficits are prevented by the creditors themselves.

One of the IMF's policies – forcing an export orientation on debtor nations – only increases international tensions further. For Third World exporters IMF policies are an uphill battle. More must be produced and sold at lower prices. But lower prices mean less revenue and hence less progress towards paying back debts.

Third World developing economies are also competing now with the former Comecon countries of central and eastern Europe. In Germany it can be expected that financing the economic, monetary and environmental union between East and West Germany will mean further interest increases because capital market demands will rise considerably.

European Monetary System (EMS)

Within the European monetary system the German central bank (Bundesbank) contributes to balance of payments inequalities within Europe by its calculated undervaluation of the Deutschmark, which is achieved through interest rate policies that are relatively high for the European Community. High German interest rates attract capital from the other countries. Our neighbours are forced to respond by raising interest rates, too, or by agreeing to devalue their currency within the EMS.

The adjustments actually necessary for currency parity are always considerably delayed because they reflect a loss in government prestige. West Germany profits from this imbalanced situation because German exports are inexpensive in foreign countries and sales can be increased, whereas European imports in West Germany are relatively expensive and are increasingly replaced with domestic products. This is how the famous 'world export champion' developed. But, this mercantilistic illusion will someday be costly, because the necessary elimination of balance of payments surpluses could affect many jobs in the supply and export industry.

The Green Party calls for an international economic policy of co-operation that can lead to a settling of balance of payments inequalities within an acceptable timeframe. The political risks involved in a crisis of confidence in the banking industry and stock markets have been underestimated – not only by the Green Party.

With roughly one million employees making up four per cent of the former West Germany's work force, the financial sector is one of Germany's key industries. In 1950 its share was only two per cent. Its growth rates are still far above the averages in other areas of the economy. Financial accidents will therefore have significant repercussions for the entire economy.

Bank failures, the US savings and loan scandal, and the stock market crashes of 1987 and 1989 are not simply inconveniences for a wealthy minority. Collective wealth, such as health and life insurance and pension and union strike funds, and those of churches and other non-profit organizations are also invested in the market and threatened by instability. Unclear liability conditions such as dealing in futures or securities of questionable worth (like junk bonds), as well as insufficient functioning investment protection and supervisory systems, could bring financial ruin to the majority of the population in a matter of seconds.

Whether an 'accident' in the financial system can be brought under control by *ad hoc* arrangements, or whether it will expand into an international depression as in 1929, also depends on the general climate and the trust that the majority of bank customers and investors have in their financial institutions. The following draft of Green policy approaches focuses on four areas of a new financial order:

1. international co-ordination of macro-economic policies (financial, monetary and fiscal policy);
2. the regulation of banks and financial markets;
3. supervision of national and international securities markets;
4. the elimination of debts and alternative development financing.

An ecological global economic order based on solidarity

The economic defects outlined above are detrimental to international economic policies aimed at ecological equilibrium and a socially just economic system. The predominance of financial transactions over trade and economic development and the increasing distance between the worlds of finance and real goods conceal immediate economic priorities. We believe that a reversal of this situation is needed. Financial transactions must be integrated into a foreign economic policy based on solidarity. Banks and stock markets should see themselves as supporting the reshaping of international economic structures. As 'craftsmen' they are welcome, but their attempt to take an architect's role in building a stable and just international economy proves fatal.

Nevertheless, the creative powers of an international credit system must not be lost. We reject an undifferentiated critique of external-debt financing as well as calls for re-establishing the gold standard or a monetary system where money and goods are exactly matched. Instead we seek to distinguish between 'constructive' and 'destructive' financial developments. Modern financial instruments ought to be employed, while potentially destabilizing, purely speculative transactions must be prevented or reduced.

Feminist theory on the symbolism of money
The development of Green strategies for relativizing the all-mighty power of money is based on the feminist analysis of the symbolic meaning of money. Placed in its social context, money is not a simply neutralizing mathematical unit. Instead it represents particular social values like eternity, wealth, and luxury. The consequent development of a money-based economy was accompanied by a dramatic shift of social values, recognizing only pluses and minuses that can be expressed in monetary terms. This has meant that most of the domestic work performed by women is not accounted for in the statistics measuring economic success in industrial societies. Women's work has systematically been devalued as the monetarization proceeded. Our financial system therefore effectively supports a patriarchal reality.

This type of analysis can be expanded to cover ecological and social values more generally. One logical political step is to include the so-called 'external' and social costs of industrial society in the gross national product calculations to make the damages caused by production visible. In the German parliament, the Green Party has taken the initiative here, calling for the inclusion of ecological and social costs in national accounting. Expressing the costs of environmental damage in financial terms, however, has its limits. The price of irreversible destruction, for instance, cannot be calculated. The loss of species from tropical rainforest destruction cannot be reversed by replanting programmes. Thus new economic thinking demands greater public awareness of non-monetary economic factors.

In numerous Third World countries basic needs are met through subsistence and barter economies that are excluded from GNP calculations. These countries are then falsely characterized as 'underdeveloped' and increased industrialization is mistakenly called for. For us this phenomenon is yet another example of the questionability of the GNP as an index of prosperity .

Qualitative indicators such as 'domestic work' expressed in terms of hours per day or year; information on energy use in production; per capita sulphur dioxide and nitrous oxide emissions; and balances of poverty and wealth must be presented along with the national accounting sums of traditional economic GNP calculations. This pluralization is a valuable starting point for Green policies, which can be further developed with the goal of questioning the power of the financial world and the magic of money from the inside.

International co-ordination of macro-economic policy

Since the mid-1980s the 'group of seven' industrial countries has met periodically to discuss international macro-economic conditions and policies. In 1985 they concluded the so-called Plaza Agreement and two years later signed the Louvre Agreement. However, in their meetings and agreements on monetary and fiscal policy, public debt and desirable adjustments of exchange rates were established on a strictly voluntary basis. Although only fragments of the agreements were published, the actual economic developments show far from satisfactory results.

In 1984 an alternative effort, The Other Economic Summit (TOES), was founded. TOES is working on an alternative programme of macro-coordination and, from a Green perspective, presents promising approaches.

We want to see stronger co-ordination of international macro-economic policy with binding international agreements that should be delegated to an internationally legitimated body. A 'world economic council' analogous to the UN's Security Council should be established with representatives from the main economic regions: the Americas, Africa, Europe, and the Pacific Basin. Permanent and rotating chairs could be established in this council to help make up for the discrepancies in economic power.

The new world economic council would have two main tasks. The first would be co-ordination of macro-policy, but this does not mean international fine-tuning. It is much more important to prevent countries and regions from working against one another and over longer periods creating imbalances that supposedly benefit individual economic powers. Appropriate sanction mechanisms must be developed, such as penalty interests for countries with permanent surpluses.

The second task would be international co-ordination of ecological policies. The world economic council should help overcome the previous lack of co-ordination or any conflicts between environmental, fiscal and monetary policies. The council should develop a plan for reconciling ecological and economic policies. In the long run this council could also be granted authority to make decisions on international liquidity. Prerequisite to this, however, is clear democratic approval beyond that of economic and finance ministers; new forms of democratic participation must be developed. (See also Chapters 2 and 3.)

In the long run regional economic discrepancies must be so drastically diminished that the world can eventually arrive at an integrated international economy with a common monetary and financial system or a 'federally' organized central world bank. From a short-term perspective, a multi-centred economic system would be a step up from the post-war hegemony of the United States.

A stable international financial system must grow and mature over time. Stability cannot be achieved by majority decisions at the UN level. Just as US hegemony allowed the independent economic development of Western Europe and Japan, these new economic centres should now actively support the development of further regional centres.

From the EMS to an all-European Monetary System
What are the consequences of our long-term perspective for the further development or reshaping of Western European regional financial markets? According to the analysis in the preceding chapter the EMS has increasingly turned into a Deutschmark club. The Benelux countries have closely linked their currencies to the Deutschmark, and the Delors plan also clearly recognizes the power of the German central bank.

If this situation does not change, the Bundesbank will in fact – though not necessarily by mutual agreement – assume the role of a European central bank because of its ability to determine monetary policy for EC member countries. The Bundesbank favours an option along these lines and seems less and less eager to institutionalize a regionally based European central banking system similar to the US Federal Reserve System. Its willingness to discuss compromises ends when the independence of the new European central bank or its single focus on price stability are questioned. We reject this Bundesbank policy because it reinforces economic asymmetries within the EC, directly contradicting the idea of an integrated European community in a world economy based on solidarity.

The economic and monetary union currently pursued by EC Council members is moving in a direction that the Green Party cannot support. As planned, the European central bank would be exclusively concerned with monetary stability. It could thus undermine attempts to conduct ecologically and socially responsible economic policies in individual EC countries. The

German central bank insists that a European central bank be given powers to operate completely independently of governments and parliaments. The political union of the EC would thus be prepared and preceded by the economic and monetary union. This will realize nothing more than the 'primacy of the economy'. The most powerful capital interests will take precedence over policy interests.

At a time when the Comecon bloc is breaking up and its individual European members are moving closer together, forced integration into the EC monetary union, and later to the EC political union, means no more than that these states will be pushed into the associated EC member status for some time. They will become a 'second class Europe', and the opportunity to create an all-European economic order will have been wasted.

As an alternative, the Greens support further development of the EMS to avoid the disadvantages discussed above and to smooth the way towards an all-European economic order based on democracy and social equality. National financial and monetary policies must once again become the subject of political debate. Central bank policies must become accountable to democratically elected parliaments when it comes to how they simultaneously take into account the requirements of ecological and foreign economic equality, meaningful work for all and a just income and property policy. We therefore support the legally guaranteed pre-eminence of economic and monetary policy decisions made by parliaments and governments, without, however, legitimizing their access to the currency printing presses.

The EC's monetary system must make a constructive contribution to the establishment of an all-European monetary order. Counter-measures must be taken against the currently emerging DM-fixation in Eastern Europe, which was intensified by the monetary union of the DM and the East German mark. One possible approach would be for EC members and East European states to work out a system similar in conception to the EMS. Fixed, but periodically adjusted exchange rates between 'West' and 'East' could be installed and guaranteed with the establishment of an intervention fund by Western Europe while appropriate reforms in Eastern Europe are going on or are underway. Its point of reference could be the European currency unit (ECU). This system could gradually be fully developed into an all-European economic order.

The independence of an integrated all-European monetary system must be guaranteed in so far as the European financial policy must not be placed in the service of national or European budget deficits. At the same time there must be agreement on sanction mechanisms to eliminate structural and lasting balance of payments surpluses.

Regional and ecologically oriented monetary policy

Regional disparities, intensified by traditional financial policies, are a central challenge to the EMS as an all-European monetary system. Regarding the instruments of monetary policy, we think it worth exploring ways that traditional policy (minimum reserve requirements and open market operations) can be expanded and fine-tuned to include regionally specific policy instruments.

Regionally oriented monetary policy should support and speed up the process of regional economic rapprochement between the 'core countries' and economically weaker members. For instance, the European central bank could engage in open market operations which give priority to debt notes issued by an economically weak country. Thereby, international (EC-wide) demand for that country's debt papers would rise, allowing it more flexibility in choosing economic policies.

As long as national central banks exist, similar institutions could, as a first step, be devised on a regional instead of national basis, targeting monetary policy instruments much more precisely. For instance within West Germany there are relatively large regional discrepancies. Because the Bundesbank implicitly targets the most diversified and economically strongest regions while neglecting different regional effects, these differences are often accentuated rather than softened by monetary policies.

Related ideas on 'regionalizing monetary policy' were discussed in the United States at the beginning of this century, when the establishment of the Federal Reserve System threatened to end all regional autonomy. It may be worthwhile to take a new look at these discussions.

Limits on capital transactions

Within the EC and all of Europe, unilateral measures (capital controls) to overcome large economic discrepancies should be allowed, particularly for Portugal, Greece and Spain. Even with a single monetary area, limitations such as legal restrictions on foreign purchases of vacation homes and other property by non-residents and majority share-holdings of domestic corporations could be established. As with the housing credit subsidies or capital formation laws in West Germany, these countries should also be given the freedom to establish specific interest ceilings to support regional or structural developments.

On a more general level we believe that monetary policy should be relieved from being the isolated domain of financial elites inaccessible to the public. Advisory councils should be established to formalize discussions and exchange among monetary policy-makers, union representatives and non-governmental organizations including environmental groups, consumer advocates and the Third World solidarity movement. A dialogue would be organized between the goals and political ideas of the grassroots movement and those of high finance. It should go without saying (but doesn't) that equal representation of men and women in all leadership positions and in all policy planning committees must become a top priority for all reforms of the monetary authorities.

Regulating banks and financial markets

While the international banks expand their global presence with increasing strength, there is no institution which keeps track and is able to evaluate the developments of financial markets as a whole. For instance, the explosion of new financial instruments in West Germany between 1986-88, where so-called 'swaps' increased from 2 billion to 230 billion DM, took place without the Bundesbank even offering a political assessment. The public is faced with these astounding figures and nobody seems to know or care if they are good or bad.

We think that a financial market supervisory board should be established to observe and evaluate trends in international financial markets. The supervisory board would be an important link between macro-planning and financial institutions' credit policies. We see this supervisory board as providing important services to the World Economic Council proposed above.

Although a number of private and (semi-)official institutions currently follow developments in international financial markets, none of these is mandated to interpret its findings for policy purposes. In particular, there is no mediation process currently taking place between financial market trends and macro-economic policy-makers. Obvious signs of allocative misalignments – capital flight, tax evasion, insider scandals, excessive speculative take-overs, extreme over-valuation of certain financial papers and so on – must be reported and stopped through international agreements.

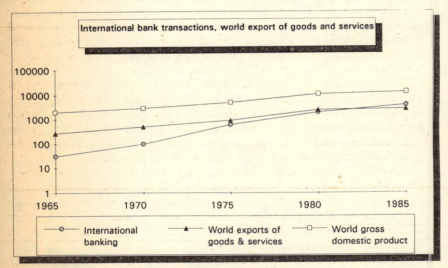

International Financial Intermediation, The Brookings Institution, Washington, D.C.

We believe that a high priority must be placed on slowing down the extreme increase in capital mobility and the explosion of financial innovation. This can be achieved only by a policy focused on slowing down capital mobility that will force financial managers to calculate more carefully the risks and benefits of capital transactions.

To strengthen financial stability we support measures that several prominent economists have called 'throwing sand into the gears'. These include taxing short-term foreign exchange transactions, increasing minimum reserve requirements for foreign exchange bank accounts and strengthening legislation on non-resident accounts. The supervisory board should not be solely responsible for such policy initiatives. Instead, EC institutions and other regional agencies should also be encouraged to develop initiatives and if necessary apply them unilaterally.

The principle of reciprocity can only apply to equal partners. Individual countries or groups of countries must be allowed to apply selective controls to capital transactions. Developing countries especially must be permitted to install one-sided capital controls (for example, reduced profit transferal, interest equalization taxes) to guarantee their independent development. On another level, international agreements and tax treaties on income from wealth must be established.

Networking supervisory boards at the multilateral level

The financial supervisory board proposed above should also have to work closely with national and regional bank and stock market supervisory institutions. While the latter generally limit their attention to banks and financial papers directly under their own jurisdiction, contact with an international agency would be an important way to keep them informed of international developments. This currently takes place only on an *ad hoc* basis. The Bank for International Settlements (BIS) provides some of these services and should be integrated into the United Nations' framework. It is also possible to conceive of the transformation of parts of the IMF for these functions.

International co-operation has existed in this area for quite some time, at least among industrial countries. The so-called 'Cooke Committee' operating within the Bank for International Settlements in Basel was the leading institution for negotiating international standards for minimum capital requirements. These standards have meanwhile been accepted as the norm for credit institutions by national bank supervisors in the western OECD countries.

The BIS also offers international regulators a forum for discussions on new financial instruments. It also offers an informal institutional framework for co-operation which in many instances may be all that is required for a smoothly functioning world financial market. It is, however, limited to a small number of countries. This limitation should be lifted and the idea of the BIS should be expanded to include all UN members.

Binding international treaties are urgently needed in some areas and cannot be replaced by informal agreements. Legislation on money-laundering from drug and illegal arms trading is necessary as well as controls of other illegal cross-border financial transactions (capital flight). The same goes for multinational corporations' financial transactions that should be separated from the non-financial business and submitted for bank supervision.

On the EC level, several legislative initiatives to increase the effectiveness of bank supervision have been launched by the European Commission in Brussels. The so-called second bank directive established among other things the principle of host country control. This may help fill some gaps in the current supervisory system.

Host country control means that the jurisdiction of each national bank supervisor extends to all banks based in its territory and to these banks' activities abroad. In other words the Federal Supervision Office for Credit Systems (BAK) in Berlin will supervise the Deutsche Bank in West Germany and all its foreign branches and subsidiaries consolidated in the Deutsche Bank Corporation.

Several supervisory gaps remain nevertheless, as some financial centres base their comparative advantage precisely on the right to secrecy. These regulatory loopholes should be closed by amending current legislation and intensifying co-operation between national supervisors and the International Financial Market Supervisory Board mentioned above.

The EC directive on reporting requirements is also a step in the right direction, as it increases the disclosure requirements of private financial institutions. Given the speed of change and the range of bank activities, however, the new legislation chronically lags behind the actual situation. A radical extension of public disclosure both on a national and an international scale is necessary along with improved public access to statistical and other information on bank activities.

Bank supervision, consumer rights and anti-trust policies

Bank supervision is weak because its legal applications are too narrowly defined and completely detached from anti-trust law considerations. There are in effect no functioning anti-trust policies. The power of banks is greatly enhanced by the uncontrolled wave of bank mergers, joint ventures and other co-operative agreements among banks. These effectively amount to a strategy of dividing up markets among the largest banks as a deliberate bank policy.

There is also no legislation to prevent or control the establishment of 'financial supermarkets' combining insurance with banking and other financial services in one institution. Virtually no legislation ensures the institutional separation between offering credit for risky investments and then providing risk insurance for these credits.

Here, as in many other areas, current supervisory rules neglect the consumer's interest. There are some EC initiatives to incorporate consumer credit rights in the body of bank legislation, but these initiatives leave much to be desired. It is especially necessary to develop more stringent insolvency guidelines for individuals and to establish consumer counselling institutions to deal with individual over-indebtedness.

On the national level in Germany we believe that fundamental reform and improvements in the available in-house expertise of the Federal Bank Supervisory Agency (BAK) is necessary. The BAK must become an agency that can act independently of the Bundesbank. Currently an office of secrecy, the BAK should instead feel responsible for providing a publicly visible and critical opposition to the banks. Improvements in this agency's legal access to the necessary information are one aspect of needed reform. A second important reform aims at incorporating consumer protection and public information on the banking industry into the tasks of the bank controller.

A catalogue of measures limiting the economic power of large banks is also urgently needed in Germany. Banks are able to conduct industrial policy, undermining public, regional and national economic policy. The 'general business conditions' – the basic terms of business to which all customers must agree – are currently determined by the banks themselves. They should be reviewed and made federal law, but rewritten to protect consumer interests.

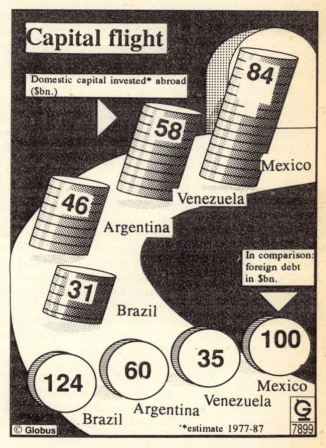

Capital flight

Domestic capital invested* abroad ($bn.)

84
Mexico

58
Venezuela

46
Argentina

31
Brazil

In comparison: foreign debt in $bn.

124
Brazil

60
Argentina

35
Venezuela

100
Mexico

© Globus

'*estimate 1977-87

G 7899

The federation of German banks (Bundesverband deutscher Banken) must be publicly reviewed for possible violation of the laws of competition. These federations are dominated by large banks which use them to obtain information on their competitors and are able to influence interest rates and other prices for financial services.

It is also necessary to prohibit bankers from becoming directors of non-bank client corporations and to outlaw the bank's proxy voting rights and holding of non-bank assets. Ethical principles must become part of official bank policy, and banks must abide by international codes of conduct, particularly in Third World countries (see Chapter 6).

Stock market supervision

The stock market crash in autumn 1987 made it clear that co-operation among international financial markets is far from satisfactory. The same is true for stock market supervisory agencies. In its current form, the International Organization of Securities Commissions in Montreal is little more than an *ad hoc* committee. Several of its member countries, West Germany among them, do not even have a national stock market supervisory agency. Instead, West Germany is represented by the self-nominated 'Working Group on German Stock Markets' which is closely tied to the large commercial banks and can hardly represent an independent position.

The establishment of an independent national supervisory agency must be the first step towards reforming the structure of national securities markets. This newly created agency would be the national representative in any international association of stock market supervisors.

Supervision of the securities market must end the currently tolerated conflicts of interests among banks, traders and listed enterprises. The dominating role of big banks as investors and as traders in the German stock exchange must be disclosed and limited so that new decentralized structures can develop. Regional stock markets for small and middle-sized businesses and municipal credit currently on the decline should be supported.

A number of initiatives have been taken to improve co-operation among national stock markets on the EC level. These include 'the investment guideline', 'stock exchange sales offers' and 'insider trading' agreements. Experience shows that the piecemeal approach of translating EC directives into national law one by one is going ahead without a clear overall concept for the reorganization of European stock markets.

The European Community has totally ignored the fact that in recent years a wave of bank consolidations has made new regulations necessary. We support reshaping merger controls to take the special characteristics of the banking sector into consideration. This means in particular, accounting for the cumulative effect of small shares in many segmented markets. EC-wide levels of intervention should be set at lower than the national levels. We think that a five per cent market share should be a limit for bank mergers in Europe. Limiting bank mergers would tone down the battle currently taking place over the 'number one' financial centre in Europe. This struggle between Paris, Frankfurt, London and Luxembourg leads to an unnecessary and dangerous deregulation race.

End big bank domination

In West Germany the large banks in Frankfurt lobbied hard to establish futures markets, and pushed for increasing liberalization in order to rival other European financial centres.

In our opinion the main reason for the general sluggishness and inefficiency of German stock markets is big bank dominance over virtually all areas of the securities business: issuing and trading securities as well as the system of proxy voting rights concentrated in the hands of the banks.

As there is neither competition in the underwriting business nor independent market supervision, access to information on company performance, market conditions and other relevant data is extremely expensive and involves large time lags for the public and even for many institutional investors. Investors are therefore forced to rely exclusively on the word of large banks. No independent authority provides a check against fraud, insider trading or even excessive transaction prices. Furthermore, shareholders' meetings of large companies are in most cases dominated by a few large banks which hold significant shares either directly or indirectly via proxy votes of the investors.

A reform of German securities markets must start out by reducing the power of large banks on the one hand and building up an opposition on the other. The securities business must be fully integrated into the body of anti-trust legislation. Moreover, a national (public) agency supervising the securities markets must be established, and securities markets must keep their status as public institutions, rather than private enterprises.

All information relevant to securities markets, including the annual reports of stock market companies, must be accessible to the public free of charge (for instance at savings banks or public libraries). Reforms of corporate law and bank legislation are necessary to ensure adequate rights for consumers and for small investors in particular.

Third World and Eastern Europe: debt reduction and alternative development financing

In the preceding chapters we have discussed the devastating effects of the debt crisis and the resulting transfers of capital from South to North. Global and comprehensive debt elimination is the only possible way to reverse the prevailing resource drain, which is the most urgent problem of international financial relations. Only debt cancellation can free debtor nations from making foreign currency for debt servicing the focus of their policies, in the pursuit of which they unscrupulously sacrifice natural resources and the social and cultural development perspectives of their populations.

Refusing debt elimination could, in isolated cases, be used as an economic sanction in combination with other sanctions. There must, however, be political justification and proof that such a sanction is absolutely necessary.

The Green Party has always advocated a general debt moratorium on all interest and principle debt payments, followed by an international debt conference for the general reduction of outstanding external debts. As with the London debt agreement of 1953, which was of great benefit to the West German economy, this conference must start with the assumption that much outstanding debt is simply not repayable.

From the creditors' side it must be recognized that the majority of existing debt claims today are illegitimate on the grounds of negligence in bank lending policies, widely fluctuating interest rates and increases in real interest rates. Risk was thus shifted exclusively on to the debtor countries. Moreover, accounting rules on international debt benefit only the banks. The lack of international agreements of what constitutes bankruptcy and regulations for the banks to write down sovereign non-performing debts has favoured the creditor. Last but not least, the ready acceptance of fugitive money by capital flight money deposited by rich individuals and firms in the same banks that hold claims on the countries of origin presents a particularly ironic twist to the debt crisis.

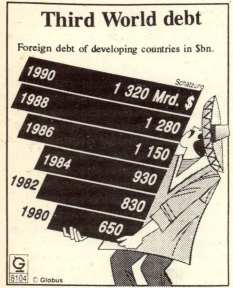

Third World debt

Foreign debt of developing countries in $bn.

1990	Schätzung
1988	1 320 Mrd. $
1986	1 280
1984	1 150
1982	930
1980	830
	650

G 8104 © Globus

Several lessons can be learned from the Third World debt crisis. One is that an international law on bankruptcy must be established, one that defines 'national insolvency' in economic terms. Secondly, the implicit subsidies provided by the taxpayer to private commercial banks must be ended. In the past the subsidies have taken the form of services provided to the banks by the IMF, the World Bank, the Paris Club and other official agencies. Thirdly, there is a need critically to evaluate the effects of certain techniques of granting bank credits (syndicated loans, variable interest rates) with respect to asymmetries benefiting the creditor.

In West Germany we support a reform of the corporate tax law to prevent banks from receiving tax credits by placing credits on the balance sheet as 'uncollectable' items without having to prove that they are actually non-performing assets. This technique of 'silent reserves' has allowed the banks to write off large portions of Third World and Eastern European debt at the expense of West German taxpayers without providing relief for the debtors.

An international debt reduction conference must simultaneously suggest methods for future development financing in a global economy based on solidarity and ecological change, plus come to binding conclusions. The above mentioned measures, the co-ordination of international environmental and macro-economic policies, and regulation of financial markets (banks and securities markets), provide a general context for reforming development finance. They offer the basis for a stabilizing of interest rates and prices, as well as the elimination of international imbalances founded in industrial nation power politics. Both are necessary prerequisites for improved chances for development.

Development: a quantitative to a qualitative definition

Experience over decades of 'development' has shown that development policies cannot be adequately defined quantitatively. The United Nations set a contribution of 0.7 per cent of gross national product as the amount of development aid that should be contributed by each member country. But setting quantitative goals such as this can actually be counter-productive given the limitations of traditional aid policies that only operate on the basis of development projects and do not question the global economic framework. Such goals force investment without taking the quality of a project into account.

It is a fact that many bilateral and multilateral development projects and programmes have actually been damaging, sometimes deadly, because they followed an unecological, world market-oriented Western modernization strategy. There was no consideration of natural and cultural situations or of a country's independently formulated development goals.

Our alternative to the quantitative definition of development is a qualitative one. This means we question the entire 'project approach' because it cannot match the dimension of the actual problems. Qualitative development policies create a political and economic framework that allows countries to introduce independent and environmentally sound development for the basic needs of most of their populations. We refer to what Third World theorists call 'self-reliant development'.

Self-reliant development means above all a break from the current fixation on the export-oriented world-market development logic that industrial states dictate to developing countries. We do not want to replace world market integration with autarkic states. Rather we want to see development turn towards domestically oriented economics in regional associations. The goal must be regional self-reliance for basic goods. Production for the world market is of only secondary importance.

This goal can be supported through development of efficient regional financial systems and capital markets, subsidies for small businesses, grassroots social services and professional education.

Qualitative development also costs money. Speaking from a 'North' perspective, however, it follows this basic principle: taking less is better than giving more. First, the drain of financial resources from the Third World to the industrialized North must be stopped. To place development financing on a more solid basis we must employ the entire spectrum of available means. When assessing sources of financing to be mobilized over a long period of time, domestic and foreign factors must be considered separately. Financial sources include the entire spectrum of internal savings, unilateral foreign government transfers, long-term credit guarantees at market prices or concessionary conditions, as well as private direct and portfolio investments. Some basic principles and policy guidelines are sketched below.

Mobilizing internal financial sources: 1. The ability to raise local savings must be increased. This means that a decrease in consumption appropriate for each social class must be made possible. The state must be able to levy taxes which take more from the rich than from the poor.
2. Real interest rates (that is, what is left when inflation is accounted for) must be structured to encourage savings.
3. To motivate potential investors, expected rates of return on investment projects must be higher than the interest on savings deposits.
4. The state must be willing and able to spend tax revenues on development to meet basic needs, and to prevent the 'self-servicing' by the corrupt elites.

External development financing can support this mobilization of domestic capital sources through building and expanding local (national) financial markets, banks and savings institutions. The industrial states can make a direct contribution to this by negotiating limits for the repatriation of their TNCs' profits and by discouraging capital flight motivated by tax evasion and the illegitimate appropriation of government funds by corrupt politicians.

When searching for misappropriated funds or exposing illegal weapons accounts, drug money, and so on, co-operation between authorities can be organized by supervisory agencies in co-operation with banks. As financial transactions are in fact much more personal than banks make them out to be, instituting controls in these areas is actually quite easily done. In other words, the banks usually know where their clients get their money from. The trick is to develop guidelines forcing international banks to respect national laws.

External development financing: 1. It is essential that international interest rates and price levels are calculable for Third World debtors. Large unexpected fluctuations in international interest rates and prices bring increased risk and reduce capital expenditures.
2. Industrial countries must increase net unilateral transfers for development financing.
3. Investing in developing countries must be made more attractive relative to investing in the financial markets. International investors must expect a rate of return in developing countries higher than that from international interest on deposits.

As mentioned above, government development funds should not be linked to the quantitative 0.7 per cent goal. The cost of development must derive from a qualitatively new strategy for an ecological global economy based on solidarity, one that offers the Third World better conditions. Elements relevant to costs in this newly defined setting include bilateral co-operation, on the one hand; on the other hand, increased funding will be needed to strengthen international agencies, such as UNCTAD and UNEP, that especially benefit the Third World.

In the long run we favour multilateral over bilateral development finance. These two approaches should add up to about one per cent of the gross national product.

In addition there is a completely new task: the financing of the Environmental Fund that would offer financial compensation to Third World countries abstaining from the use of local resources for ecological reasons (see Chapter 2). The Greens support a national contribution of approximately one per cent of the annual GNP for this fund. Thus the total costs of new strategies of qualitative development add up to about two per cent of a country's gross national product.

New challenges to humankind – global climate protection, preserving tropical rainforests, water protection – place new responsibilities on Third World countries especially. Financial help is more than an act of solidarity, it is in the direct interest of the North and its peoples. The survival of all depends on preserving and protecting tropical forests, and is threatened by their deforestation.

The means for development financing must increasingly be transferred to the multilateral level. At the same time donor funds should no longer be granted as credit, but instead should be non-redeemable contributions. On the side of the recipient these supports, mediated by a multilateral fund, could take the form of low-interest loans.

We reject the allocation criteria of bilateral co-operation motivated by foreign policy interests. These buy 'good conduct' (like UN votes) from as many recipient countries as possible by giving everyone 'a piece of the pie'. Allocation criteria must be reoriented to securing basic needs, and culturally and ecologically sensible and sensitive development.

At the same time that we reject the UN's goal for development financing of 0.7 per cent of GNP, we criticize the way the German government reaches – or fails to reach – this goal. For years its contribution to development aid has been a maximum of 0.4 per cent of GNP funding, systematically short of the agreed-upon amount. In addition this reduced contribution has only been achieved through 'mixed financing', combining private credits with public payments. These credits help meet the planned goal even though mixed finance credits require trade contracts between 'giver' and 'taker'. These obligate a recipient country to purchase technology or goods from the donor.

The Greens cannot accept this abuse. It is actually a hidden subsidy for German exports. In addition, West Germany has not adhered to the parliament's decision to focus development aid on rural development, the fight against poverty and support of the least developed countries, especially those in south-Saharan Africa. Instead it gives preferential treatment to industrial development in the so-called 'threshold' countries of South-East Asia and Latin America (known as 'newly industrialized countries' or NICs in World Bank terminology).

New methods of multilateral development financing require a fundamental restructuring and democratization of multilateral development institutions. This will especially affect the work of the IMF and World Bank, as well as their increased integration into the structures of the UN.

Over the last two decades these institutions have conducted a reckless policy of impositions on debtor nations that has caused widespread suffering. The national sovereignty of developing countries has been systematically disregarded, an indignity spared the very countries that are most responsible for the financial imbalances – the USA, Japan and West Germany.

International Monetary Fund and World Bank complicity with private banks was reflected by the cocktail parties at their annual assemblies – financed and organized by big banks. We support a return of the IMF to the task laid out in its articles of agreement: financing 'short-term' current account deficits. As outlined above we must be sure that structural adjustments take place in countries notorious for their trade surpluses. The voting rights of the currently penalized Southern national groups must be improved to the point of parity. Long-term imbalances cannot be eliminated by either the IMF demands for world market-oriented structural adjustments or the World Bank's commensurate financing facilities.

Above all, the World Bank should end its one-sided world market profitability orientation and work in a more decentralized way. We propose shifting its focus to regional institutions for Africa, Asia and Latin America, formed around funds rather than credit institutions. There should be close connections with the corresponding regional development banks.

Foreign private investments have a two-sided nature. On the one hand Third World countries cannot realistically do without the technology and know-how from the industrial states. On the other, their need increases the danger of dependency on foreign providers of capital who destroy the recipient country's independent right of self-determined development. This conflict of intent can be solved only if exact regulations for foreign investment are developed.

The expected rate of return for foreign investors must be higher in developing countries than that from investment in a 'savings account' on the international financial market. Government subsidies of transnational corporations' private investments – and their safeguarding with capital protection agreements (as is done by the German government on a bilateral basis) – is, however, not a suitable method of support, because it only benefits the investor. This type of government protection makes the decision easier for corporations to withdraw their money via profit transfers from the country on short notice.

Small businesses by contrast are typically less mobile and more likely to be interested in networking with domestic suppliers and buyers. Potential small investors must be granted a certain amount of 'legal safety' for business conducted abroad which is not yet well developed.

We call for eliminating all direct investment subsidies for large enterprises. Capital protection agreements must not be allowed to establish unequal contracts with one-sided advantages for the foreign investor, as happens with current German government practices.

Alternatives are the structuring of bilateral agreements in the form of draft contracts, as developed by the International Center for Settlement of Investment Disputes (ICSID). Another alternative is offered by the complete substitution of bilateral processes with multilateral agencies, such as the Multilateral Investment Guarantee Agency (MIGA), a daughter organization of the World Bank.

MIGA must, however, be reformed so that the equal participation of 'North, South and East' will be secured and access will be possible only for small businesses. Also in need of reorganization is the German system of publicly funded international chambers of commerce, which should have a broader and socially representative membership.

5. An ecological all-European economic order based on solidarity

Role of the European Community in the world economy

A reorientation is needed

The development of supranational structures in Europe is in principle the best response to the decreasing decision-making abilities of the old nation states. Increasing internationalism in politics, economics and culture forces smaller countries especially either to work together or cede their rights of sovereignty to supranational organizations or regional associations of states. And many current challenges to society – global warming, North-South problems, the prevention of global war – extend beyond Western Europe and Europe as a whole.

The West European approach to integration, namely the European Community (EC), has, however, developed in such a way that many people have come to doubt the fruitfulness of (West) European integration. The integrated market is mainly oriented towards the interests of the industries in the core countries and has not benefited all countries and social groups involved.

The EC treaties place a one-sided emphasis on the integration of markets, making the European Community a community of corporations. Because of its emphasis on corporate interests, the EC is incapable of meeting the challenges of regional and global solidarity.

In the 1990s, economic relations within the EC can no longer be understood in terms of foreign trade. Regional industrial and especially agricultural policies are increasingly subject to Community policy instead of agreements between countries. For this reason West German foreign trade policy with respect to other EC countries can be spoken of only in a limited sense. This has meant that Germany's EC neighbours are less able to avoid the effects of its economic dominance.

Germany's key role within the EC is clearly expressed in its special political and monetary position. The deutschmark has taken on the function of a reserve currency within the European Monetary System (EMS), effectively placing monetary control of the entire EMS in the hands of the Deutsche Bundesbank (German Central Bank). No EMS member can avoid the effects of the Bundesbank's restrictive policies.

In areas essential to the creation of a real European Community, the EC merely practices policies that ensure market integration.

* This applies to environmental policies, which at the EC level have long been limited to cases where unilateral efforts in environmental protection could have potentially restricted the freedom of inter-community trade. True, the 'goal of environmental protection' was written into the EC treaty with the Single European Act of 1986. But this did not lead to independent environmental policies of equal importance to European market policies.
* As long as market integration policies continue to intensify the sometimes crass differences in regional levels of development, regional policy conducted by the EC is very limited in its effectiveness. Despite statements to the contrary, the EC's current approach causes a weakening of regional independence and diversity.
* EC social policy exists only in its rudimentary beginnings. A concept for community-wide minimum social standards has no chance in the current set-up.

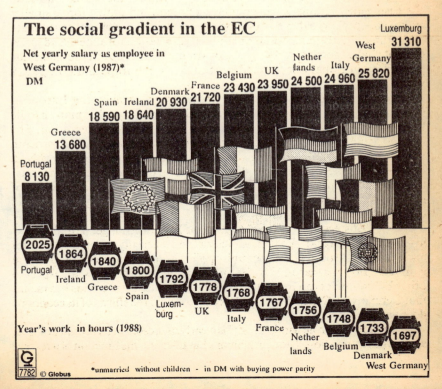

The social gradient in the EC

Net yearly salary as employee in West Germany (1987)* DM

Luxemburg 31 310
West Germany 25 820
Netherlands 24 500
Italy 24 960
UK 23 950
Belgium 23 430
France 21 720
Denmark 20 930
Ireland 18 640
Spain 18 590
Greece 13 680
Portugal 8 130

Year's work in hours (1988)

Portugal 2025
Ireland 1864
Greece 1840
Spain 1800
Luxemburg 1792
UK 1778
Italy 1768
France 1767
Netherlands 1756
Belgium 1748
Denmark 1733
West Germany 1697

7782 © Globus   *unmarried without children - in DM with buying power parity

Despite considerable authority, above all in the area of economic and trade policy, and a constant expansion of EC legislation, the EC acts without sufficient democratic legitimacy. The European Parliament's powers are very limited. The Parliament does not cast decisive votes on any of the important EC legislation. Legislative power is effectively in the hands of its member countries' governments. The Council of Ministers has authority over key decisions.

The EC is in urgent need of fundamental federal restructuring. It must in particular reform its goals and democratize its decision-making structures. Improvements in foreign trade policies as outlined elsewhere in this book are not to be expected from an EC which, with the support of the EC treaties and largely unchecked by democratic controls, has carried out policies in the interests of large European corporations.

We think that the EC's goals must be reformulated, moving the priority from economic integration to environmental protection, social justice and international equality. With respect to these goals, the EC policies of the EMS, the liberalization of capital transactions and the harmonization of indirect taxes all need to be revised (see Chapter 4).

Democratization must lead to a permanent broadening of the rights of the European Parliament, which should take over responsibilities from the Council of Ministers and the Commission. Furthermore, the national parliaments of member states should be granted rights, extending from participation in parliamentary discussions to veto rights. This democratization should also include institutional strengthening of regions, including states, as well as more direct participation by citizens and non-governmental organizations (NGOs).

Increased handling of neglected tasks at the EC level raises the danger that citizens will become alienated from an increasingly anonymous decision-making process. The EC should be restricted to formulating EC legislation (directives), allowing room for independent regional policy-making. During this process the importance of the national states will inevitably decrease.

The emerging possibility of an all-European unification encompassing East *and* West should force the EC in the foreseeable future to question its own structure and place this matter before all of Europe for discussion. We do not share the opinion frequently voiced by EC bureaucrats and politicians that the EC can serve as a model for a future European-wide unification.

An all-European society must be able to integrate, in a non-discriminatory way, social and economic systems that differ even more than those the EC has brought together. Closing the gap in living conditions must be the goal and not the prerequisite of this integration. Democratic participation in decisions affecting all of Europe cannot depend on whether or not a country is economically developed enough to keep pace with the standards of the West European domestic market.

EC foreign economic policy

The EC has made Western Europe the world's largest trading power. The West German economy is one of its driving forces. Until 1990 the EC's trade surpluses almost always equalled those of the Federal Republic because the balance of payments of the other eleven member countries are predominantly negative or only somewhat balanced.

As the EC integrates economically towards a single market, its size allows for greater economies of scale. It improves the industrial and technological basis for increased competition with other global regions. Interest in forming similar commercial unions also exists in other parts of the world. With this the danger increases – if not to world peace, then to the development of stable, co-operative world economic relations. The problem does not lie with the creation and differentiation of world trading regions, but rather in their aggressive commercial policy orientation.

With respect to non-members, the EC acts to a large extent as a bloc. EC treaties have transferred considerable responsibility in this area to the Community. Nevertheless, there is still leeway for member countries' independent policies, such as export credit guarantees and 'voluntary' restrictions on imports.

In quantitative terms the most important foreign trade relations that the EC maintains are with the developed capitalist countries of the OECD. These account for most of the Community's foreign trade, and are also the Community's most intensive competitors for future markets and key technologies.

Although the EC propagates the ideology of free trade, and stresses that it does not want to cut off other countries from the internal European market, its real policies follow EC interests, pragmatically making selective use of both free trade and protectionist methods. Compared to the current situation in Germany it is an increase in protectionist tendencies.

EC market barriers against more efficient competitors include anti-dumping tariffs. These are also applied to products produced within the EC with considerable imported components. The EC also applies non-tariff barriers to trade, such as technical norms, at a time when they are being abolished within the internal EC market itself.

If we criticize the EC's tendencies towards selective partitioning of markets, then we do so because it concerns the protection of less competitive industries within the framework of an overall aggressive foreign trade policy. The protection of ecological and regionally appropriate domestic policies must be possible to safeguard these policies from negative external influences.

The development of the internal European market poses a great threat to the economic self-determination of neutral northern and central European countries (EFTA member states) that do not want or are unable to become EC members. EC countries are by far the most important export markets for all of these countries, thus they are unconditionally forced to conform to EC market regulations. We think an appropriate policy response would be to grant these countries, regardless of their membership status, the right to participate in decisions that concern their vital interests.

The EC's economic relations with the former Comecon countries are at present organized by bilateral agreements between individual nations and the EC. The EC is by far the most important Western trading partner for the former

European Comecon nations, whereas for the EC these trade relations are of relatively little significance.

The enormous debt of most of these countries further exacerbates the imbalance. With the help of bilateral treaties the EC has handed out rewards of varying magnitude for the introduction of economic liberalization measures. This policy means that these countries are associated to the EC on its conditions. It is foreseeable that these countries will fall out of the 'frying pan' of the Soviet Union and into the 'fire' of complete EC dependency.

In Central Europe and many Third World countries, economic relations with the EC are more important for them than for the Community. The creation of the European single market will clearly impede the access of Third World countries to the European market. The EC has preferential trade relations with many African, Caribbean and Pacific nations through the Lomé Convention. In Lomé IV, agreed upon in 1991, the preference system was pushed to the background by an emphasis on more competition and a policy of structural adjustment.

The Lomé Convention contains among other things the STABEX, which has proved to be an insufficient instrument for stabilizing income from raw materials. It suffers from far too little funding and is not suitable to stop let alone turn around the worsening terms of trade. It can even out and balance the price fluctuations of exports, but not change the general downhill slide. Although the Lomé Convention does contain some positive approaches, in its current form it holds the associated countries securely in their function as suppliers of raw materials rather than helping them out of this role.

Some EC agreements with Third World countries contain regulations beneficial to developing countries. But for the most part they are set up to develop or hold foreign markets open for the EC under the most favourable conditions possible, and to secure the EC's sphere of influence. Independent of these interests, access to the Lomé Convention must be open to all Less Developed Countries (LDCs). STABEX and SYSMIN (see Glossary) must be further developed in such a way that they do not create competition, but rather bring about a meaningful replenishment of the International Raw Materials Fund (see Chapter 3 and Appendix 2).

When it comes to newly industrialized countries that produce industrial goods in competition with EC commodities, the EC follows a clearly protectionist policy to impede their market access. The same is true for agricultural importers. In this area the EC protects its markets from competitive food imports and leaves the Third World countries often only the option of producing livestock feed for the EC. At the same time, via export reimbursements, the EC subsidizes the prices of its own agricultural exports and thereby undercuts world market prices.

Accompanying this policy are the food aid shipments to a number of poor countries which continue to use up agricultural surpluses and serve to open markets for EC products. As long as the EC sticks to its discriminating foreign trade policy toward Third World countries, it is clear that even the best development concepts will be in vain (see Appendix 3).

Demands on EC policy for the world

The future of Europe will not be decided in Europe only; and Europe can influence its own future through its behaviour in the greater world. As an exceedingly prosperous and productive community, the EC has the opportunity and, as a group of nations that includes the most important former colonial powers, also the historical responsibility to take a leading role in reordering world trade relations.

This role includes moving international agreements towards an ecological world economy based on solidarity and going beyond this by taking independent initiative. A global orientation must not stand in the way of taking local and regional action, and vice versa: such action should not obscure a global orientation.

North-South differences, just as the changes in Eastern Europe, challenge EC policies on the domestic as well as international level. The temptation is great to hold back funds for global co-operation and use them for domestic purposes. Such a policy, which only consolidates an island of wealth in the EC, should be firmly rejected.

Corresponding to its responsibilities in foreign trade policy, the EC's growing role in development policy and in environmental protection means that the implementation of the guidelines presented here must take place at the Community level. It would be a step forward for the EC to commit itself to the orientation developed here so far (see Chapters 2, 3 and 4). But EC-Europe's necessary role in the forefront does not end here. It goes on to include a contribution to the international establishment of the principles of ecologically responsible global trade and economic policy based on solidarity.

East-West economic relations

The development of economic relations with Eastern Europe was a key element of social democratic policies of détente. Confrontation was to be replaced by co-operation, change achieved through rapprochement. What was the result of the economic co-operation that began with West German treaties with Eastern European countries in the early 1970s?

Until 1990, economic co-operation between East and West Europe was very limited, compared to that within Western Europe. There were only a few cases of joint production. Trade co-operation was structurally unequal: West German machinery and equipment traded for Eastern raw materials, furniture, textiles and agricultural products. The Federal Republic's economic policy towards some Comecon countries was increasingly limited to more or less uncontrolled loans in Western currencies, without considering the planned investment projects themselves, or their long-term profitability and possibilities for repayment.

This lending policy led to enormous debts in Yugoslavia, Poland, Hungary and East Germany, with no solution in sight. The gap between the Comecon countries and Germany widened during the 1970s and 1980s in levels of material standard of living, production technology and international competitiveness.

East-West economic policies since the early 1970s were unable to stop the spiralling weapons' build-up or prevent the deterioration of superpower relations after 1979. The economic situations in Poland, Rumania, Yugoslavia and Hungary – countries receptive to efforts at détente – are even more catastrophic than they were 20 years ago. The Soviet Union's ability to provide for its population has also not improved over the last 20 years; it has instead enormously worsened.

With hindsight one can see that the careless granting of Western credit in the 1970s was a substitute policy for necessary reforms on both sides.

In Eastern Europe the necessity for thorough economic reform was widely discussed in the 1960s and partially begun, in Hungary for example, or in Czechoslovakia during the Prague Spring of 1968. During the period of re-Stalinization thereafter, now politely referred to in the Soviet Union as 'the period of stagnation', the movement towards economic reform was reversed. Its supporters were forced to resign or go into exile.

In many Eastern European countries the structural deficiencies and incompetence of the 'real socialist' planned economy were concealed by Western loans. The population was temporarily better supplied with consumer goods, the shortage of spare parts alleviated by imports. Despite this investment, machinery and production facilities became ever more out-dated. The poor co-ordination between the different economic branches was not changed by Western credit – just the opposite.

Large Stalinist heavy industry projects financed with Western credit – oil refineries in Rumania or steel works in Poland – intensified the structural problems. Because of shortages of raw materials, suppliers and processors, many of the large factories lie unused or operate at partial capacity.

Consumption based on imports collapsed. Even former Polish Communist Party members openly admit today that the jumbo West German credit of those days was a 'trauma'. No one knows exactly where the funds flowed. Walesa spoke of a double-edged gift to Poland's economy. Western loan policies have contributed to the fact that the Eastern European countries must now make basic economic reforms under much worse conditions than in the 1960s.

The policy of 'credit instead of reform' was apparently a comfortable way out for the ruling elites in Eastern and Western Europe, especially West Germany. Instead of creating a new basis for relations with the Third World (North-South) after the oil crisis, they distributed petrodollars worldwide in the form of loans. In the face of the oil price shock and the social reform movements in Eastern Europe, the money was naively used as an all-purpose cure, instead of considering ecological and social reform of the industrial system in East and West. Today this can only be seen as irresponsible.

The widespread assumption in the West that the Soviet Union would accept liability if problems with repayment arose in its realm (the so-called umbrella theory) does not say much for the quality of Western government foreign policy advisors.

In terms of the resulting intensification of the economic and social crises in Eastern Europe, and divergence of East and West Europe, the East-West economic policies of the 1970s and early 1980s cannot be considered good policies in the interest of domestic and global peace. The monstrous military investments made within the framework of NATO's double-track resolution should not be forgotten when evaluating this economic policy. Both East and West allowed the arms race to prevent civil co-operation and conversion from becoming the focus of their policies.

Serious economic crisis in the former Comecon countries

The serious crisis in the former Comecon economies has meant that their own people are structurally under-supplied and that their products are no longer competitive on the world market. In the 1960s the USSR had hoped economically to 'catch up with and surpass' the United States. It must have been a great shock when, in the 1980s, Soviet products could no longer compete with those from the newly industrialized countries – South Korea, Taiwan, Singapore, Brazil and Indonesia.

Similarly the US watched as Japan rose to become a major economic force on the world market. Along with the progressing integration of the EC countries, this has led to a multi-polar world economic network. The military – especially nuclear – polarization of the superpowers has been historically overhauled by the altered multi-polar world economy.

With the election of Gorbachev as General Secretary of the Soviet Communist Party, a policy of reform began once again. This reform has been taken up at different speeds and in various ways by all of the East European countries. The Greens are following these reforms with hope and sympathy. Our expectations are high for the ability of the people to effect the necessary changes themselves. The only chance for a socially and economically attractive future lies in a lively democracy with public debate, demonstrations and free votes to determine which path to take out of the economic crisis.

Despite inspiring beginnings, we see that at the same time, even in the USSR, the reforms have not yet gained the social strength necessary to solve the material, ecological and psychological problems of the Soviet Republics. To date the USSR is far from having a political or economic federal concept that guarantees decentralized decision-making and provides guidelines for state legislation. Nationality conflicts heighten supply bottlenecks and prevent necessary structural changes in the economic and social order.

Poland established the political basis for comprehensive economic reform after forming an all-party coalition government under Mazowiecki that included Solidarity and the Communist, Farmers, and Democratic Parties. Mazowiecki relied on the market economy and took the bitter path of subjugation to the IMF's conditions. It is following Hungary's course, but with a considerably worse availability of goods.

The social and human costs of this austerity policy are very high. Cancelling subsidies means higher prices. Indexed salaries and retirement benefits lag behind galloping inflation. People often do two jobs in an inefficient infrastructure with poor consumer goods. Poverty and unemployment increase with no unemployment benefits available.

This situation shows that the reformers have not accepted their social responsibilities. In the face of economic misery they are not able to develop socially acceptable reforms. The hope placed in the 'beneficial' effects of the market economy by Eastern governments and opposition movements often seems naive, given our political understanding and knowledge of the market economy in capitalism. This belief in the market economy seems anachronistic judged by what we know about the relationship between economic and political power, as well as the need for restructuring industrial society.

While we consider the ecological and social restructuring of Western market-oriented industrial society – and in West Germany this discussion has also reached critical thinkers among the Christian Democrats and business sector – we see the readiness in Eastern Europe to believe in the 'self-healing ability' of the market. This shows that little is known of the massive waste and misallocation of resources in market economies, or the conflict between economy and ecology.

The Greens assume that ecological damage in Eastern Europe is even more widespread because of the serious disregard or contempt for nature in Stalinist thinking, and massive industrialization. Thus an adequate reform policy must from the beginning develop a new social and political relationship to nature. The introduction of market economics alone cannot guarantee an ecologically and socially structured economic order.

The question of the role of women in society and the terrible double-burden that women in Eastern Europe bear is also not discussed by reform communists in terms of moving to eliminate sexual discrimination in the distribution of labour. Instead, the old solutions of 'woman as housewife and mother' are offered. Although we wish Gorbachev's reform policies success, as the best possible solutions for the Soviet Union under current conditions, we cannot forget our objective criticism. We have faith in the learning process in Eastern Europe, already increasing in the independent democratic movements.

Eastern Europe and the West: crisis and reform policies

Crisis and reform in the East also affect the West; ecological catastrophes do not stop at political borders. Water and air pollution or radioactive contamination cannot be stopped by tanks, missiles or the most modern weapons system. The explosion at Chernobyl certainly proved that we cannot depend on the 'superiority' of Western technology.

The Russian civil rights campaigner Lev Kopelev, currently living in exile, predicted that if Gorbachev's reform policies failed there would be a civil war in Russia. A civil war in a country bursting with atomic missiles and nuclear power plants, like the USSR, is no internal matter. It would be a catastrophe of global proportions.

The social crises in Eastern Europe also concern the West. The doubts of people who see no future for themselves in their own countries will affect those who are so much better off only because they were born 'on the right side of the wall'. There will be either an influx of refugees, or new anti-Western populist movements. We have already seen the beginnings of these in the USSR and Hungary.

The ever-growing dislike of foreigners stands in the way of opening the European Community. This 'common European home' will remain an unrealized utopia if its Eastern 'wing' explodes.

The central question as to whether the chance exists for civil social structures to develop will remain unresolved in the face of poverty and unsolved supply problems that lead to individual violence and martial law.

In this situation the West German government and major parts of the Social Democratic Party pursue a double-pronged European policy. On the one hand they want to strengthen the centralization and independent strength of the EC through the European single market and Franco-German military co-operation. Hidden within this concept is the tendency to take away economic policy 'breathing space' from the neutral and non-aligned positions in Europe and to build a West European 'fortress' capable of competing in international politics and the world economy with the US and Japan. On the other hand they take up the idea of the 'common European home' and strengthen their contacts with former Comecon countries.

These are two contradictory concepts. They could probably be made compatible through the readoption of Adenauer's 'magnet theory' in which the West is further strengthened, so that it can pull Eastern Europe towards it like a magnet. Military thinking is substituted by economic thinking aimed at increasing influence. This thinking and method of action is focused on linking Czechoslovakia, Hungary, Poland, etc. to the EC by association or membership while excluding the USSR. However, the all-European concept requires inclusion of the USSR and changing the present EC of twelve states into a decentralized European-wide federation.

At the heart of West German interests in the Comecon countries is the hope of tapping new markets in the face of the structural growth crises of Western industrial nations. Further, they hope to open and enter these markets under economic conditions about which West German managers rave ecstatically: markets where the consumer still really needs something, in countries so politically disoriented that they cannot set restrictive ecological or social guidelines.

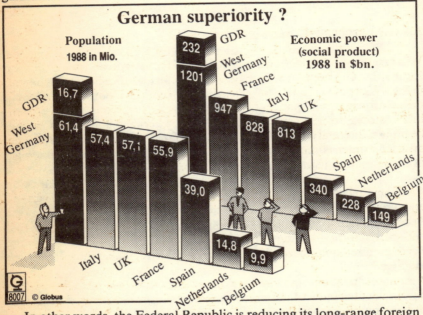

German superiority ?

Population 1988 in Mio.

Economic power (social product) 1988 in $bn.

GDR — 16,7
West Germany — 61,4
Italy — 57,4
UK — 57,1
France — 55,9
Spain — 39,0
Netherlands — 14,8
Belgium — 9,9

GDR — 232
West Germany — 1201
France — 947
Italy — 828
UK — 813
Spain — 340
Netherlands — 228
Belgium — 149

8007 © Globus

In other words, the Federal Republic is reducing its long-range foreign policies to foreign trade interests. This will prove dangerous for Europe as a whole, because it depends on the export of the Western economic model as if there were no discussion over its destructive ecological and social consequences. It depends on the export of Western industrial, labour, and agricultural methods which are speeding the destruction of our social and environmental resources in so many ways.

West Germany has not yet developed any ideas for solving the economic crises in Eastern Europe that question our destructive consumption patterns and lifestyle. A rational, well-thought-out policy would be oriented towards improving the supply of goods to the public while reducing environmental damage and energy use in their production.

Only an industrial policy that combines ecological and social standards with economic criteria and helps to avoid our wasteful and self-destructive lifestyle deserves political support. An industrial policy that damages the European continent even more, like the dams and power plants planned by the Hungarians and Austrians for the Danube, calls for joint resistance by ecologically oriented movements and parties.

For West European industry, Central Europe is a prospective 'work bench', offering low wages and social costs as well as minimal union rights. Already Polish farmworkers are coming to West Germany as if the tradition of Polish seasonal workers in German agriculture remained unbroken since the nineteenth century. Once, these workers came with German citizenship from Silesia. Later they came as Polish forced labour. Today they include teachers and doctors who need Western currency to survive.

An All-European Economic Community

What are our proposals? At present, because of the intensified crises in Eastern Europe and Gorbachev's reform policies, there is a chance for a new chapter in East-West political and economic relations. Our idea is not that the export-oriented foreign trade policies of West Germany and the EC now simply expand into Eastern Europe. Rather we are interested in seeing that the relations will be politically equal and the economic strength of West Germany will not be misused to intensify cultural and political differences or to create a new type of economic dominance or even dependence. We hope to see:

* economic relations that are part of an all-European disarmament, conversion and peace policy that also includes the US;
* economic relations that provide room for the development of democratic and social reforms in Eastern and Western Europe;
* economic relations that will reduce ecological burdens and increase energy savings;
* economic relations based on ecological and social responsibility for the development of industrial societies instead of the short-term profit interests of some multinational corporations or the self-interest of central-planning bureaucracies;
* prevention of a climate catastrophe, in the interests of the survival of human societies.

How can this be achieved?

Key to a new quality in East-West relations are economic and political reforms in all Eastern European countries. Without fundamental democratization of political life and without turning away from the complete power of the bureaucracy there will be no way out of the crisis. The democratization of domestic political debate leads to a desire for change that opens better perspectives for life and work.

The rapid changes in the Comecon countries and the Soviet Union show that their societies are themselves attempting to shape their interests. At the same time it becomes clear how strongly 'actually existing' socialism suppressed dissent within its plan and command economy. The reason for the return to national values and autonomous utopias is found here, as in Lithuania.

A country made up of many peoples, the USSR is no federalistic republic or confederation of states. The economic misery of the centralized, industrial planned economy has accelerated the decline of the central state. The republics of the USSR are forcing market economy decision-making structures into the political and economic arenas. The pressure to abolish the planned economy stems from the companies' inefficiency, no longer tolerated by the people. All hopes are concentrated on the market economy, seen as a way to set limits on the power and inefficiency of decision-makers.

The Greens maintain that the economic changes taking place in Eastern Europe require ecologically based guidelines. The swing from a planned to a 'free market' economy will bring painful losses in income, and, without ecologically based guidelines, increase the rapid decline of areas already seriously damaged by air, water and ground pollution.

The Greens are looking for stronger political co-operation with independent movements in Eastern Europe which trace the ecological catastrophes back to industrial growth economics.

The capitalist market economy is good at improving the efficiency (labour productivity) of factory units, however day by day it endangers the survival of future generations. It also has the tendency to concentrate power in market structures. In this process of reform, we see a basis for co-operation between critics of Western lifestyles and consumption and East European reform groups, if the industrialized world of the North recognizes that there is only one world, and that the questions surrounding the survival of the South must be tackled.

Over the short-term, dialogue with Eastern European countries must centre on agreements and aid that will make a peaceful and democratic reordering of society possible. The many demonstrations and elections in all Eastern European countries, as well as public debate and controversy, create the hope that the internal strength of their societies will bring forth the perspective for a better way of life. The West can make this long path easier and open all-European perspectives on co-operation.

An all-European economic order will be possible only if militaristic East-West opposition is transformed into an all-European security system. The 2 July 1990 economic, monetary, social and environmental union of East and West Germany was actually the integration of a Comecon country into the EC. German responsibility for the effects of World War II, from which the USSR suffered, requires that Germany consider the economic and ecological development of the Soviet Union as one of our concerns. The economic opening of the EC to all Eastern European countries as outlined above is the appropriate answer to the problem of how to overcome East-West military opposition.

Disarmament in both East and West offers the possibility that military use of resources will be replaced by social policies that can lead to a better society. For this it is imperative that the military blocs disband and form an all-European security system.

Many existing structures could be extended for building the all-European economic order. These include:

* the regional economic areas of the EC, EFTA and OECD, which are increasingly co-operating;
* the European Council, which has set a standard for democratically constituted countries in Europe with its many conventions, especially in the area of human rights;
* the United Nations and its Economic Commission for Europe (ECE);
* the March 1990 CSCE economic conference, and beyond.

With the EC agreements ceding rights of sovereignty, the EC is the only international organization that has placed countries within an economic policy that envisions an (EC) internal market.

The ECE supplies economic analysis and data for Europe. The CSCE economic conference creates a framework for discussion, but does not develop perspectives for an all-European economic order.

Possible role of the European Council

The European Council's structure, previous areas of responsibility and conditions for access make it a suitable forum for all-European co-operation. Its current institutions include the Committee of Ministers (government level) and parliamentary assembly (parliamentary level). It is open to all democratic states in Europe. Several Eastern European countries are currently becoming members.

The European Council must be strengthened and expanded in the following areas: all-European responsibility; its capacity to make decisions and take action; democratic legitimation and financial support. The parliamentary assembly should meet year round, with its representatives elected by popular vote.

After the parliament's authority is expanded, the Council can play a key role in establishing guidelines for a unified Europe. The European Council's budget must be adequately funded so that the parliamentary assembly will be able to work on the numerous core areas of all-European policy such as:

* democracy and human rights;
* peace and security;
* independence of regions and peoples;
* economic structures;
* the calling of a European conference on debt;
* European environmental standards;
* European development fund;
* Europe and the 'Two-thirds World'.

The USSR is part of this Europe. An all-European economic order must develop structures that allow for its economic integration. The all-European economic order must meet the prerequisites and requirements for the process of growing together.

The CSCE conference provided a first step towards an equal dialogue over economic questions. The European Council offers a decision-making structure in which this dialogue could continue. The greatest impediment is that the

EC is quite reluctant to question its current decision-making methods and mechanisms. To realize European-wide prospects, Western European structures must be changed and opened.

The CSCE conferences offer a framework where all-European structures for security, economic, ecological and human rights questions can be proposed and agreed upon by consensus. Their implementation can be carried out by the European Council, the ECE economic commission of the UN, or a new institution of the CSCE itself.

Here it is important that in the area of security policy, both the West and the East abandon 'bloc thinking' and support an all-European security order. An all-European security system co-ordinated at the political level by agreements of the CSCE has a chance to succeed only if the creation of an all-European economic order is part of the deal. Here, it is necessary that Eastern European countries are offered the opportunity to receive non-discriminatory entrance into the EC internal market.

The Cocom lists that impede East-West trade must be eliminated immediately. The modernization of Eastern Europe's industry and service sectors requires its complete access to the latest energy and environmental technologies. Military conversion on a large scale is realistic only if it is ecologically and economically viable to rebuild outdated industrial facilities for the production of consumer goods.

All-European Conference on debt, and a financing concept

The founding of the European Bank for Reconstruction and Development (EBRD) by 41 countries with 20 billion DM in start-up capital is an indication of the urgent need for investment in Eastern Europe. The debate with the US over Soviet participation was finally decided in the USSR's favour.

The fact remains that the founding of this bank is not a sufficient response to the overwhelming debt problems of East European countries. The interest and repayment on debts from the failed industrial expansion policies of past decades, especially at times of high interest rates, frustrate political efforts to stop urban decay and promote infrastructural and industrial production possibilities that have popular support and offer hopeful new perspectives for life and work.

The German government should call for an all-European debt cancellation conference in the framework of the international institutions (CSCE, IMF, ECE, EC). It should politically regulate the foreign debt problems of Central European countries. This initiative would complement the important role of the London Debt Conference after the Second World War, which reordered and effectively eliminated German war debts. Poland and Hungary, for example, require a comprehensive cancellation of foreign debts as an indispensable prerequisite for future action.

Debt rescheduling offers a breathing space but no solution for deeply indebted countries. The Western banks and governments share the responsibility for most of these debts, because the productive use of officially guaranteed loans was obviously not analysed. Political criteria were the guiding principles, rather than economic efficiency.

There must be a comprehensive cancellation of national and private debts in countries like Czechoslovakia, Poland, Hungary and Yugoslavia. Private banks have to inform the public about outstanding debts, showing the amounts already written off. That is because banks save taxes when they depreciate bad debts, thus the tax-payer pays part of uncollectable debts.

The remaining residual claims should be transferred into ecological funds in the currency of the country where a fund is located. These funds should be exclusively used to rehabilitate ecologically damaged areas like the Danube, the Vistula, the Oder, the Bay of Danzig, the Baltic Sea, or for modernizing outdated industrial facilities. Participants in the funds should include social and ecological representatives.

Establishment of an All-European Development Fund

The formation of the European Development Bank does not offer a sufficient financial basis for the enormous demands of Eastern European countries. The slow death of Lake Baikal and the Aral Sea, damage to forests in the Erz mountains, air pollution and the destruction of landscapes in the coal mining areas of Kattowitz, Cottbus and Leipzig, heavy metal pollution in the Elbe and Oder – these are only the best-known environmental problems. Energy use per person in Eastern Europe is sometimes higher than in Western Europe. The main cause of air and water pollution are hopelessly out-dated industrial facilities that have high energy losses and are kept going by chronic capital deficits.

The expected influx of Western capital offers a chance for technological modernization of these industries and thus a chance for short-term reduction of the causes of the most extreme environmental problems. At the same time, however, the danger exists that with the creation of investment incentives, employment problems and alleged economic viability arguments will undermine environmental standards. The economic and social crisis will be played against the environment.

Moreover, increased environmental stress is to be expected as the East takes over Western market economic models of production and consumption. This will range from an explosion in garbage production to the expansion of atomic energy and transport policies that favour individual transportation of persons and goods rather than the expansion and renewal of public transportation systems.

Therefore an ecological restructuring programme for Central and Eastern Europe is necessary, as well as for a unified Germany. The Western countries should finance a revolving all-European development fund. Payments into this fund would be adjusted according to an individual country's ability to pay. Funds would be allocated according to the principle of 'one country – one vote'. They should be distributed by a credit co-operative or public bank.

The European Council could be the decision-making body for this fund. It should be used to finance areas often avoided by private investors, but ones crucial to the development of an all-European infrastructure and the protection of our life-supporting environment – from the Baltic and North Seas, to preventing carbon dioxide emissions.

In every Eastern European country there is a real and enormous need for public sector investment to finance an infrastructure that can meet basic demands. Areas in need include: transportation, energy, supply channels, sewage treatment and communication. The development fund can provide financing for such projects. Funds should be distributed in an investment offensive to build a functioning infrastructure, placing equal value on both social and ecological criteria.

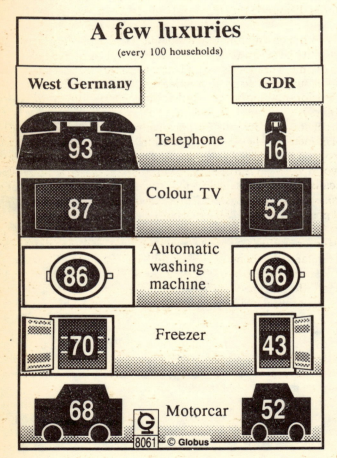

A few luxuries
(every 100 households)

West Germany		GDR
93	Telephone	16
87	Colour TV	52
86	Automatic washing machine	66
70	Freezer	43
68	Motorcar	52

8061 © Globus

Construction of decentralized energy supply facilities supported by energy saving investments in the production and housing sectors could be an example of political guidelines that successfully tackle the reordering of Eastern industrial society.

Prospects for an All-European Monetary Fund

The twelve EC member states have set up a plan for their monetary union. Whether this plan will be carried out or not depends on many opposing interests within the EC countries. The disagreements between the policies of the German Bundesbank and the monetary policies in France, Italy and England are so great that it is not clear whether economic and monetary union will be achieved.

We think that an all-European monetary fund should extend beyond the EC (EMS) and the EFTA countries. The support fund should be used to guarantee exchange rates. The financing of the support fund should be conducted so that countries with export surpluses pay proportionally more into the fund. This would dismantle the structural imbalances between various regions in Europe.

Only with such a multinational monetary understanding can the complete convertibility between all European countries be achieved in a reasonable amount of time. The monetary fund must be democratically structured so that past export surpluses do not determine the amount of influence a country has in the decision-making bodies. Rather the principle 'one country – one vote' should apply.

The constitution of an all-European monetary system alone will limit and control monetary policy-makers in their individual decisions. Creation of an all-European monetary fund is justified because we already live in a multi-polar world, between Europe, the US and Japan, as well as South-East Asia, and because the dollar is increasingly losing its function as a base currency. Our task is to make the Eastern European countries' entrance into the world market possible on a fair and equal basis.

East Germany's integration into the EC creates the danger that the Oder-Neisse-Line, reunified Germany's eastern border, will become a foreign trade border similar to that between Mexico and the USA. The EC's trading borders should not be allowed to be so discriminatory. The EC must meet the economic and social differences between Eastern and Western Europe with open political borders. Separation will only renew East-West differences.

6. Controlling transnational corporations

The economic power of transnational corporations

Transnational corporations (TNCs) are among the strongest forces shaping international trade and international economic relations. They are involved in the exploitation of natural resources and contribute directly to ecological destruction. Moreover, in many countries, TNCs manipulate strategic aspects of national and regional economic policies. Transnational corporate policies are a major obstacle to an ecological world economic order based on solidarity.

The economic influence of TNCs in the international economy increased considerably during the decade of the 1980s. As this trend went hand in hand with a wave of mergers among large corporations, the economic power of individual corporations is greater than ever before. Instruments of control, on the other hand, have failed to keep pace, and the public accountability of TNCs has declined.

These trends are true for the world as a whole and within the European Community and other OECD countries in particular. Corporate expansion has created a situation where most markets are dominated by a small number of leading firms that compete with each other only as a formality. It is an irony of history that the 'free market economy' has become such a powerful driving force in Eastern European economic reforms, just as the catchword 'big is beautiful' is becoming the slogan of a new type of private capitalist planning.

During the 1960s and 1970s TNC investments in Third World countries were hailed for bringing about the technological transfer considered key to economic development. It is true that some LDCs were able to reach a position of international competitiveness in motor vehicles, electrical goods and consumer electronics. But unless they were able to transfer these technological advances into the domestic sector of their economies, the advantage proved to be short-lived. During the 1980s in particular, transfers of profits back to the industrial countries exceeded local gains.

It was not only the debt crisis and the inevitable ensuing political instabilities that reduced the interest of TNCs in further investments in the Third World. Other considerations led to the retransfer of parts of production, and especially of research and development facilities, back to the industrial countries. At the end of the 1980s, Third World countries found themselves in an extremely weak position *vis-à-vis* foreign investments. And in contrast to the early 1970s their bargaining power was diminished, a situation that must be taken into account when discussing possibilities for control over TNCs.

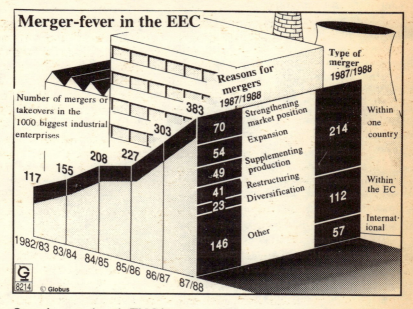

Merger-fever in the EEC

Number of mergers or takeovers in the 1000 biggest industrial enterprises

117   155   208   227   303   383

1982/83   83/84   84/85   85/86   86/87   87/88

Reasons for mergers 1987/1988

70	Strengthening market position
54	Expansion
49	Supplementing production
41	Restructuring
23	Diversification
146	Other

Type of merger 1987/1988

214	Within one country
112	Within the EC
57	International

G 8214 © Globus

Over the past decade TNC investment strategies focused on rationalization, internal restructuring, 'global sourcing' and co-operation with other TNCs, rather than on expansion aimed at developing new markets. The necessity to increase profits by internal increases in efficiency was dictated by the macro-economic environment of the 1980s: Third World debtor nations faced severe budgetary constraints as a result of IMF-prescribed austerity programmes. In the industrial countries, conservative and anti-inflation oriented policy trends kept a tight ceiling on wage increases and depressed growth rates.

The number of mergers and joint ventures accelerated during the second half of the 1980s. Mergers resulted partly from business strategies for securing market shares and avoiding barriers to entry in foreign markets that threatened protection against exporters. Both the USA and the EC are considered potential candidates for more selective trade policies and hence were targets for transnational mergers.

In many cases, however, purely speculative motives were the driving force for corporate take-overs. There were also joint ventures and co-operation agreements for specified joint research and development or other aspects of business. Although they are directly relevant to the competitive environment, these forms of collusion are not liable for prosecution under most European anti-trust legislation.

In the areas of high-technology (electronics, communication technology, space technology), co-operation agreements between European corporations frequently win financial support by federal states. It is argued that competition in these areas takes place on a world scale rather than a regional or national one, and that Europe must fight hard to meet the challenges posed by Japanese and US companies.

The same is true in the area of financial services, where the European integrated market after 1992 provides the incentive to redefine corporate strategies on a European scale. Here, too, large mergers, co-operation and other agreements have taken place – most of which effectively limit competition.

In the United States the economic concentration that took place involved huge sums of money. Their relative size is unprecedented. The 20 largest take-overs in American history took place after 1981 and all involved $5 billion or more. The internationalization of the US economy in the context of the economic restructuring of the domestic economy also reflects the new international distribution of wealth.

Big German and Japanese corporations used their excess liquidity to purchase shares in US industry. Among these firms were Tengelmann, Hoechst, BASF, Continental, and Bertelsmann. Japanese car manufacturers, computer firms and banks also participated in a big way. All in all, foreign ownership of US assets is estimated to have reached some 15 per cent in 1989. This is less than the share of foreign assets in most European countries, but a historic high for the traditionally domestic oriented US economy.

Corporate take-overs are also a speculative fad, starting in the Western countries whose financial markets are most advanced and least constrained by regulations. The business of 'hostile take-overs', hardly known until their mid-1980s boom, arrived in continental Europe in the late 1980s. As mentioned above, the increasing availability of liquid financial resources was directly related to the less than proportional rise of wages, combined with an unprecedented surge in stock market gains. The globalization of financial markets, coupled with reduced investment opportunities in Third World debtor countries, also fostered the business of merger and acquisitions.

Conservative politicians must accept part of the blame for these developments. During the 1980s most industrial countries led by conservative governments aimed for reduced state involvement in the private sector. Privatization, deregulation and tax cuts were the new watchwords. Enforcement of existing regulations and environmental controls was relaxed. Anti-trust policies were effectively abandoned, first by the Reagan administration and then in other industrial countries, on the grounds that larger firms were justified by growing efficiency and compatibility with the principles of competition.

However, these claims are hardly reasonable. The anti-competitive nature of mergers is particularly noticeable in Third World countries. In the motor vehicle industry, for instance, multinationals divide the markets up among themselves behind the scenes to avoid 'unnecessary' frictional adjustment of their profit margins. It appears likely that a similar process will take place in Eastern Europe.

In both cases TNC behaviour deprives the host countries of the already extremely limited bargaining power that they may have used to negotiate investment conditions favourable to their national economic goals. Instead, they have to accept conditions in line with global business strategies of the TNCs.

With anti-trust and competition policy more generally, we must keep in mind the impact of corporate concentration on the effectiveness of public policies. Democratically legitimized economic policy is increasingly undermined or constrained by the corporate policies of large firms. In regions where a few large firms dominate the local economy, including small enterprises whose business is directly dependent on the central corporation, politicians have virtually no choice but to adjust their own policies to fit corporate strategies. The incompatibility of growing corporate power and stagnating democratic rights must become a central issue when it comes to economic policies dealing with transnational corporations.

Controlling multinationals

National policy instruments are by their very nature inadequate for controlling transnational corporations. While TNCs have greatly improved their internal accounting and communications systems, countervailing powers such as non-government organizations, labour unions and government institutions in charge of supervision have lagged behind.

Since the 1970s international organizations and confederations have made proposals and initiatives aimed at changing the existing imbalance of power. In 1976 the OECD issued a declaration on international investments and multinational corporations based on the International Chamber of Commerce's 1972 guidelines for international investment. A year later the International Labour Organization (ILO) agreed on a declaration on labour-related and social guidelines for multinational enterprises.

The UN Commission for Transnational Corporations, established in 1974, has been working since 1977 on a Code of Conduct with far-reaching protective rights for Third World countries. This code addresses TNC behaviour towards host countries. A general section of the code has guidelines that encourage respect for the political sovereignty and social and cultural values of the host country. These include subordinating corporate policies to the host country's development goals, non-involvement in internal affairs, and eliminating corruption. A special clause regulates contract negotiations. It should eliminate the exceptional disadvantages for developing countries associated with long-term agreements.

The draft of the UN's Code of Conduct includes most of the elements in the OECD draft: room for negotiation for individual corporate areas; protection for a country's balance of payments and credit policies; correct TNC tax payments, above all on transfer prices; disclosure of information. The UN draft, however, goes further: in social areas the principles of the ILO have been adopted. Finally, guidelines for consumer and environmental protection are also included.

The original 1977 draft was clearly designed in the interests of developing countries; these wanted an instrument for controlling multinational corporations. The representatives of the Western industrialized countries agreed to the required negotiations in order to create the necessary investment climate and to maintain stable political and economic conditions. But during twelve years of protracted negotiations they finally succeeded in watering down the draft, keeping the TNCs free of union control and achieving a 'balanced document' that Western governments, as the guarantors of stable investment conditions, could support. The greatest resistance in these negotiations came from the United States.

The UN Code of Conduct could have been much more important than other more limited declarations. But the international corporate lobby's deliberate delaying manoeuvres have prevented its ratification.

Individual attempts at corporation-wide action in the mid-1970s fell victim to the economic boom of the 1980s under conservative governments and the pressure from the European and American unions to form defensive national networks. So did the Vredeling directive, a 1980 European Parliament draft directive on European TNCs' obligations to guarantee certain employee rights to information. The Vredeling directive is expected to be renegotiated by the end of 1990.

Grassroots opposition to multinationals

Grassroots groups and non-governmental organizations around the world have become increasingly active in campaigns against the policies of specific multinationals. Groups of 'critical shareholders' have formed, using the annual shareholders' meeting as a platform for public debate of corporate policies. These campaigns are mostly concerned with such global problems as environmental destruction, racial discrimination and the exploitation of women, to name a few. International contacts exist, but they are mostly limited to a mutual exchange of information. Even the critical shareholders in the various TNCs provide at best a form of public control, but have no real decision-making powers.

The labour unions have created several institutions for better international co-operation. At the international level there is the International Federation of Free Trade Unions (IBFG) and at the European level the European Labour Union Federation. At the OECD in Paris the Trade Union Advisory Committee (TUAC) acts as a union watchdog over TNCs. At both levels there are various co-operation agreements between individual unions.

The ILO is the only UN special organization with union representation that is organized with a tripartite system that includes members of governments, unions and employers. It has completed numerous studies and introduced directives for employee rights and minimum standards of conduct for TNCs in developing countries.

The IBFG is an umbrella organization for 141 organizations and unions in 98 countries representing 82 million union members. The European Labour Union Federation links 35 unions that represent 44 million union members in 21 European countries. However, important large unions such as the CGT in France, the CCO in Spain and the CGTP in Portugal remain excluded for political reasons.

In addition there are international industry-based labour organizations such as the European Metalworkers Association; the International Federation of Chemical, Energy and Skilled Worker Organizations; the International Textile, Clothing and Leatherworkers Association; the International Organization for Professionals or the International Federation of Journalists. These and other supranational workers' organizations must not simply fulfil co-ordinational and directive functions, but should become involved in the work of international governmental organizations and institutions to bring the interests of unions and developing countries into the discussion.

The European Labour Union Federation passed a motion at its 1988 Stockholm meeting to extend the authority of labour representatives to negotiate wages on a Europe-wide scale and gain access to information on European corporations' investment strategies. These rights – including requirements that the corporations carry the financial burden – should be secured by a Europe-wide legal framework.

In response to the unsatisfactory condition of international labour rights – above all due to the pressure of the single European market – various German unions are working to establish the right to form European economic committees in compliance with the West German Co-determination Law (*Mitbestimmung*). These would present demands for information to corporate supervisory boards, via employee representatives and economic committees.

There are absolutely no European provisions for the establishment of such committees. Legal changes establishing a European corporate law systematically exclude the issue of workers' rights to participate in corporate decision-making.

Instead, German employee rights are being questioned. For instance, the fifth EC directive on corporate law that provides for a supervisory body in every joint stock-holding corporation gives those companies within the EC four models of employee representation to choose from. This directive is more permissive than current German regulation, and thus undermines workers' rights. Similarly, the tenth directive that regulates international mergers and the draft for establishing the European joint stock company are based on the fifth directive.

As a result of union efforts, worker participation committees have been established in four TNCs: at Thomson Grand Public in 1985; at BSN in 1986; at BULL in 1988; and at Gillette in 1989. These committees are, however, limited to purely information rights.

Green policy proposals

The discussion about controlling the power of TNCs can be divided into three categories: making the UN Code of Conduct legally binding; regulating social costs; and openness in corporate decision-making.

The world's top companies ranked by turnover
Conversion in DM to middle-bracketed official Frankfurter foreign exchange

1988	1987	Company	Country	Turnover	Variability(%)	Net Yield
1	1	General Motors	USA	212.9	+19	4.0
2	4	Ford	USA	162.6	+29	5.7
3	3	Exxon	USA	139.9	+ 4	6.6
4	2	Royal Dutch/Shell	UK/NL	137.5	- 8	6.7
5	5	IBM	USA	104.9	+10	9.7
6	7	Toyota Motor	Japan	98.9	+ 8	4.3
7	9	General Electric	USA	86.9	+26	6.9
8	6	Mobil	USA	84.8	- 6	4.3
9	8	British Petroleum	UK	81.2	+ 2	4.7
10	13	Matsushita	Japan	75.4	+ 9	3.9
11	10	Daimler	W.Germany	73.5	+ 9	2.3
12	19	Samsung	Korea	71.7	+85	2.7
13	12	Hitachi	Japan	68.2	+ 3	2.7
14	21	Chrysler	USA	62.4	+35	3.0
15	17	Fiat	Italy	59.9	+15	6.8
16	18	Siemens	W.Germany	59.4	+15	2.3
17	16	VW	W.Germany	59.2	+ 8	1.3
18	11	Texaco	USA	59.0	- 2	3.9
19	15	Du Pont de Nemours	USA	57.2	+ 7	6.7
20	20	Unilever	UK/NL	55.1	+12	5.1
21	25	Toshiba	Japan	52.1	+ 6	3.1
22	22	Philips	NL	49.8	+ 6	1.0
23	14	Nissan Motors	Japan	49.3	+ 5	1.7
24	26	Nestle	Switzerland	48.9	+15	5.0
25	34	Honda	Japan	47.8	+ 8	2.8
26	24	Renault	France	47.5	+ 9	5.5
27	28	Philip Morris	USA	45.7	+16	9.0
28	23	Chevron	USA	44.3	- 3	7.0
29	27	BASF	W.Germany	43.9	+ 8	3.3
30	29	VEBA	W.Germany	42.6	+10	2.8
31	38	NEC	Japan	42.3	+14	2.1
32	36	Peugeot	France	41.0	+17	6.6
33	33	Hoechst	W.Germany	41.0	+11	4.9
34	32	Bayer	W.Germany	40.5	+ 9	4.7
35	31	CGE	France	37.7	+ 5	1.6
36	35	Amoco	USA	37.2	+ 5	9.8
37	30	Elf Aquitaine	France	37.2	- 1	5.7
38	—	Mitsubishi Electric	Japan	37.2	+15	2.0
39	37	ICI	UK	36.6	+ 5	7.2
40	40	Occidental Petroleum	USA	34.1	+14	1.5
41	41	Procter & Gamble	USA	34.0	+14	5.3
42	39	Utd. & Technologies	USA	31.8	+ 5	3.6
43	43	Atlantic Richfield	USA	31.0	+ 8	9.0
44	42	Nippon Steel	Japan	30.1	+17	1.7
45	44	RJR Nabisco	USA	29.8	+ 7	8.2
46	47	Boeing	USA	29.8	+11	3.6
47	—	Dow Chemical	USA	29.3	+25	14.4
48	48	Thyssen	W.Germany	29.2	+ 4	2.3
49	—	Xerox	USA	28.9	+59	2.4
50	49	Volvo	Sweden	27.7	+ 4	5.1

Source: Suddeutsche Zeitung

Make the UN Code of Conduct legally binding: All forms of domination in international economic relations must end. All countries – particularly the smaller and economically weaker EC countries and Third World nations – must be guaranteed effective control over their own national economic development.

This implies banning all direct and indirect political involvement by transnational corporations in national policy-making. National and regional development plans must be respected. Economic activities should be planned so that environmental damage is avoided and large ecosystems are not endangered.

Economic activities of TNCs must be aimed at a fair North-South (West-East) transfer of technology and management know-how. The transfer of profits must not lead to increased debt or serious worsening of the foreign trade position of host countries. Reinvestment in the host countries should be supported.

These demands are largely congruent with the UN Code of Conduct proposal. Unions and grassroots movements must use international campaigns to pressure their governments finally to adopt the Code of Conduct and agree to deal with the questions that will arise. These questions include equal treatment for national and multinational enterprises; applying national laws instead of international law in the case of investment disputes; and refusing (foreign) TNCs the status of national corporations in Third World countries. Key aspects of the UN Code of Conduct are the fact that it is legally binding, and that it has an internationally agreed upon set of sanctions that provide incentives for TNC compliance.

Regulation of social costs: TNC investments must be evaluated and regulated according to their democratic, social and ecological implications. This means, for example, preventing social dumping through arbitrary relocation threats employed by corporations as a negotiating device to receive tax concessions or wage cuts. It also means establishing procedures for social adjustment programmes to facilitate necessary changes in economic structures.

The social costs, such as wasted resources and environmental damage resulting from the privately organized economic activities of TNCs, must be recorded and reduced. Over the long-term these costs should be eliminated by reordering production priorities. Committees should be formed from TNC representatives, local citizens, employees and local politicians to develop plans of action to achieve this. Social funds should be established, financed in part by TNC contributions.

TNC employees must be granted the best available training and union rights, meeting the highest standards. Quotas for employing women at all qualification levels should become part of the code of conduct and be enforced. For foreign subsidiaries of European TNCs, a European economic committee of employee representatives from internationally active corporations should be legally established.

Employee rights already achieved by labour unions within the EC must be maintained. We reject all reforms aimed at 'harmonizing' workers' rights or limiting them to a number of options that are below the current maximum standards in individual member countries, as is called for in the European corporation directives.

Openness in corporate decision-making: Before such problems can even be considered, it is vital that TNC policies become significantly more open. This is the only way that employees, their union representatives and the public can introduce appropriate and well-founded political and economic measures. These measures include:

* Openness in foreign relations. In Germany, we demand that the identity of shareholders be made public, regardless of the number of shares held. Members of the board of directors must be listed and the monopoly commission must have rights to corporate information. Now, it usually takes outsiders a lot of time and money to get information on TNCs. Therefore public access to corporate reports, market analyses, national reports and so on, must be guaranteed through free distribution of such information to public libraries. Free access to and wide distribution of key information should also be guaranteed in stock exchange law (prospectus requirements).

* Open annual reports. Reform of the Annual Reporting Directive is also necessary. It should detail the financial and environmental costs of the various areas of production, administration and financing. It should also include information on reserve stocks. This reform would guarantee control over transfer pricing techniques aimed at undermining national taxes or capital control.

A corporation's annual report must be further sub-divided to cover subsidiaries, affiliates and branches so it is possible for its staff, the community and local activists to assess the local situation. All TNC banking activities (for example, foreign exchange transactions) must be strictly separated from the trade and production related business. Financial transactions beyond direct payments, as well as currency speculation, must be transferred to organizationally separate or independent financial institutions.

* Eco balances. Annual reports must include a separate ecological balance sheet recording the natural resource inputs and the burden placed on the environment during production and waste product treatment. These balances should be drawn up on the basis of linear product analysis, so that the specific source of 'external' costs and damage can be determined and possible alternatives clarified.

* Social balances. Annual reports must also include social balance sheets with public information about differentials in income, working hours, working conditions, qualification and training – by country, by gender, and other relevant categories.

Compliance with these guidelines must become a mandatory prerequisite for subsidies, financial support or insurance services from public institutions like the Multilateral Investment Guarantee Agency (MIGA) of the World Bank.

Anti-trust law

In the area of anti-trust law, indicators must be developed for economic influence at the national and supranational level and the possibilities must be introduced for decartelization of large enterprises. Exceptions from anti-trust legislation should not be granted for export cartels and banks, as is currently the case in Germany. These proposals have been spelled out in more detail in Green Party proposals in Parliament for reforming national anti-trust laws and establishing multilateral EC merger controls.

The activities of TNCs should be controlled by a supranational body that must be established democratically and equipped with the appropriate authority. An EC anti-trust agency should be founded that, in co-operation with national agencies, will be able to control or prohibit large-scale inner-EC mergers.

Furthermore, not only market shares within the entire EC internal market should be considered. A rule should be introduced granting each member country a minimum 'national share' in any given market – that is, national quotas for market shares. This rule should ensure that no country degenerates into a 'satellite' economy' because its vital national markets were taken over by foreign companies through buy-outs or cut-throat competition. Unfortunately, the present development of EC integration runs counter to this proposal, as can be seen by the weak EC merger controls that have been introduced.

EC competition laws should allow for the possibility of company break-ups or for their socialization (take-over by employees), and state regulation. There may be instances where a technology requires large-scale production units that effectively amount to monopolies. In key areas of the economy (such as energy production) such concentration of economic power must be balanced by appropriate counterweights. Measures ranging from socialization to state regulation must then be considered.

Conversely, it should not be overlooked that in many developing countries the state sector assumed paternalistic control over the national economy. State regulation may therefore not be a sensible answer to excessive corporate power. This is especially true in areas like Central Africa, where there were no free-market structures of any kind to fall back on. At present, privatization of large government undertakings is rapidly taking place there, removing the burden of constant subsidization from the federal budget and stimulating private economic efficiency. The TNCs are expected to supply the capital and the corporate know-how for this process.

Given this development all the demands for more control over large corporations and efforts to develop economic democracy from below are more relevant than ever.

Political implementation

Limiting potential TNC power is the first step towards increasing and improving control over TNCs. The international implementation of our social, ecological and democratic development proposals will require political support. Unfortunately, no political constellation has placed these questions on the current agenda.

The development of an effective opposition to TNC corporate strategy will depend on unity among different emancipatory initiatives – the women's movement, the environmental movement, the peace and anti-nuclear movements, the liberation movements as well as the initiative for an ecological world economic order based on solidarity.

Initiatives of TNC employees could move things in the right direction. Regular contact at the business level and international meetings, a matter of course in manager's circles, must be supported to co-ordinate the design of opposition strategies. Citizen groups could parallel or support these strategies from the outside. A worldwide oppositional network should be established.

Only through an unfolding international grassroots' network and systematic expansion of political negotiation and co-operation can the cornerstone of an ecological economic order based on international solidarity be set in place.

7. An alternative world economic concept: strategies and alliances

Sharing the burden fairly

Foreign economic policy has always been one-sided, oriented towards national interests. This has gone so far that funds intended for Third World development have been used to promote the export strategies of domestic companies. In our opinion the structural problems on Earth and the disturbing changes in world climate call for a thorough change of course.

A shift in consciousness has also taken place, brought about by such internationally organized movements as those for peace or Third World solidarity. People are now more willing to abandon immediate and short-term interests for far-reaching and long-term considerations.

Nevertheless, we should not hide the fact that our foreign economic guidelines could bring about a noticeable reduction in our current standard of living. The German Green Party's domestic social and ecological Programme for Reshaping Industrial Society, that corresponds to this foreign economic concept, would distribute the associated burden of necessary adjustment fairly among the different groups in our society. More can be demanded from the consumption-happy middle class than from the poor, many of whom, even in the West, lack basic necessities.

But ultimately the West's poor, even when their need in most respects is due to the same causes as Third World poverty, are relatively privileged when compared to their counterparts in developing countries. The social payments they receive, even if inadequate, are also products of an economy that places the burden on the Third World. The fact that their limited funds provide them access to a wide variety of products is also related to the low world market prices for products from the South.

For these reasons, direct similarity in the interests of the poor in the North and South is absent. To ensure that the burden of economic structural adjustment to the ecological challenges will not be unbearable for particular social groups and to ensure the South's survival, necessary changes must be accompanied by a fairer distribution of wealth in the West.

A world economic policy based on solidarity can never succeed without the awareness that despite the necessary changes in lifestyle, a just world economy is in the long-term interest of present populations and their descendants.

The world's ecological crisis can be solved only if, on the one hand the maximation of profit and consumption is reduced, and on the other the social problems of most of the world's population can be relieved, especially in the Third World. For this reason it is our basic concern to stop defining 'national interest' in national terms. We must replace 'international policy in the national interest' with 'national policy in the international interest'.

Upheavals in world politics

Until recently the world still seemed to be an 'ordered' one, even if this order was precarious. The bipolarity of the political and military superpowers, the USA and USSR, paralleled the competition between two different economic systems. Within the OECD bloc, North America, the EC and Japan competed for markets, but did not lose sight of their joint interest in controlling world economics. Comecon appeared unattractive but stable. The Third World was a disputed area that offered resources, markets and strategic bases. It seemed that the emergence of China as a third pole could be integrated into the existing structure by diplomatic means.

Almost overnight the revolutions in Eastern Europe undermined this structure. The centralized government economic planning of Comecon countries had to recognize the new political competition. In the weaker countries economic competition was also a threat. The 'Second World' was now, alongside the Third World, a true crisis area.

The capitalist OECD has attempted to use the crises of the others to manage its own, and appears to have been successful. The macro-political battle over whether to incorporate the remnants of Comecon into the OECD or attempt to go beyond both neo-Stalinist command and capitalist *laissez-faire* economics to find a new independent approach will determine the framework in which alternative world economic policies will function in the foreseeable future. It seems that the first option will become reality.

The process of global reordering presents considerable opportunity – as well as risk – for establishing ecological economic policies based on solidarity. The opportunity lies in the potential to achieve peace and development; the risk lies in the potential for a new totalitarianism.

The process of democratization in Eastern Europe, despite the many resulting problems, should be fully welcomed. The Warsaw Pact nations have taken steps towards disarmament out of a serious political desire for peace as well as because their economies are too weak to support further weapons build-up. Their actions have made it possible to go from a process of international détente to peaceful co-operation. Western governments, too, could hardly continue to justify their enormous military expenditures.

Drastic reductions in military spending could free-up funds to cope with common human challenges, such as the fight against poverty in the Third World – and especially preventing the complete collapse of Africa south of the Sahara – and global climate, nature and resource protection. Peace negotiations between the superpowers can help prevent the wars in peripheral areas that have previously destroyed development opportunities in those regions.

Economic models based on solidarity, freed from current ideological relations that offer only the alternatives of state bureaucracy and Western capitalism, could mobilize the creativity and initiative of individuals or groups into a productive force without allowing them to become an elevated social class. The technical distribution of the wealth created could be left to the market after political standards are set to ensure a fair distribution.

Models must be developed that combine societal and personal demands on the market levels. This can be done by linking entrepreneurial market analysis with political resolutions on ecological and consumer policy norms. These models must free-up property and allow the consequences to follow, and recognize that true and equal freedom for all also requires equal distribution of wealth. The utopias of bourgeois society, 'Freedom, Equality, Fraternity', that developed as battle slogans against the political caprice of royalty, can be realized only in a post-bourgeois, non-capitalist global society based on solidarity.

Considering present power structures and interests, it is unlikely that the opportunities created by the collapse of a previously dominant bloc can be used to develop a real utopia. This would require the other bloc voluntarily to reject power. Despite leading politicians' declarations against exploiting the weakness of the East to the advantage of the West, their practical policies are doing just this. The Eastern European countries will be swallowed by the OECD as assets of a bankrupt estate. The destroyed economies of these countries offer strategists of economic expansion in Western corporations and governments a welcome field for growth and the final worldwide establishment of capitalistic structures. There is the danger that this historic take-over of one bloc by the other will shape all other areas of international politics for some time.

This will not only destroy the chance for development of a third alternative in the East, but will also dramatically reduce possibilities for the Third World to choose a course of independent development aimed at satisfying the basic needs of poor populations. The so-called developing countries already lack the political power to resist their forced integration into the capitalist world market.

Previously, there was at least an opposing economic and political pole to the OECD bloc, which followed its own course. But now even this limited possibility of avoiding world market competition with the far superior capitalist centres through association with Comecon countries, or even unfair trade to the disadvantage of the Soviet Union, no longer exists.

Countries are forced to co-operate with the OECD. Even a country's often unsuccessful attempt at a 'seesaw policy' between East and West to benefit its independently determined political and economic goals is no longer possible.

Effects of palm-oil cultivation on indigenous peoples

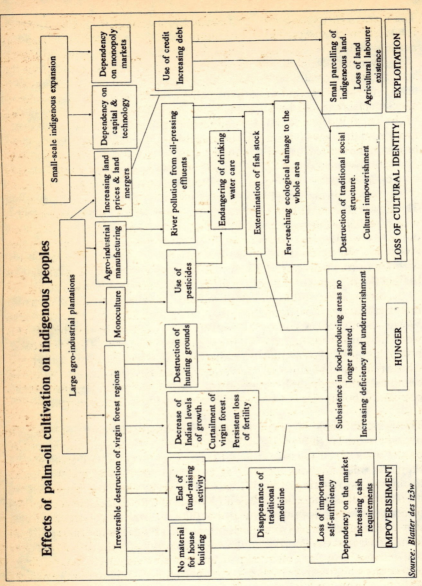

Source: Blätter des iz3w

The East, also in a state of crisis, will become tough competitors with the South for Western resources. The South, more for the worst than the better, has surrendered to the victor of the battle for hegemony between East and West.

Universalized capitalist structures would overcome blocs and replace the vertical division of the world into two highly armed hemispheres, with an earth-spanning horizontal that would subject the world's peoples to one economic and financial system and political oligopoly. The long impoverished populations of the Third World and the new paupers of the Second World would suffer most from this new division. The peace achieved in East-West relations may be lost in the battle between economic haves and have-nots.

Instead, there could be a globalization of the preventive approaches already used by emancipatory movements. In an indirect way, the emerging recognition of common life in one world would be realized within 'world-domestic' policies. The highest achievable degree of association, namely the complete incorporation of an all-encompassing global economic system, could finally focus the attention of the new world society more strongly on our common ecological dilemma. Awareness could grow that the environment can be irrevocably destroyed even without atomic weapons. We believe, however, that the political strategies to fight this danger would be impossible with the new global power structure.

If, through the worldwide establishment of capitalist structures, certain interests achieve global dominance there is a danger that poverty in the Third World – a cause of environmental destruction – could not be eliminated. This would require a thorough reordering of the world economy according to the principle of solidarity, as opposed to the 'free play of forces'. Instead, the poor, whose rate of population growth is often seen as the root of all evil, would be eliminated through population control. Current technocratic, anti-women population policy discussions show fatal tendencies in this direction.

The overshadowing of North-South policies by East-West co-operation is seen by some in the Third World as a chance finally to realize independent policies on the basis of self-reliance, untroubled by the 'development' strategies of the industrialized nations. However agreeable this idea may be, and it is similar to our own, we remain sceptical. The reduction in resource transfusions from the industrialized countries to the Third World and the associated constraints on development policies do not mean that the industrialized countries will also stop draining resources from the South on their own financial and political terms. There is a danger that, under current conditions the discussion over 'self-reliance' is nothing more than an unpromising attempt to make a virtue of necessity while the industrialized countries continue their exploitative policies without even maintaining compensation payments at previous levels.

The Greens will use their modest influence to counter the take-over of the Eastern bloc by the West, and thus counter the totalitarianism of one economic and political system. The alternative to a bipolar world cannot be the destruction of the poles, but the development of a democratic, multipolar world. The concept of 'development' must be understood in global terms.

It is intolerable that the standard of living in industrialized countries is secured and elevated while low birth rates are dictated for the Third World. The material standard of living in both North and South must be equalized at the highest possible level while taking our planet's fragile ecology into consideration. Large-scale assimilation of cultures and lifestyles, such as is caused by their convertibility into the dollar, Deutschmark or yen, must be opposed.

Alliances to build an opposition: in the South, the East and the West

The realization of a world economy based on solidarity can only be achieved by uniting widely varying political forces with similar goals and interests. The need for co-operation demands the sacrifice of small-scale goals. Directed thinking focused on the desired goal will be more productive than causal thinking, that throws back every action to the self-contradiction of the context in which it was created. The tendency to exaggerate and become lost within analysis that has grown out of the tradition of classical German philosophy needs to be expanded to include a pragmatic Anglo-Saxon orientation towards action.

Many different motivations – the will to survive, social concern, ecological responsibility or the desire for personal emancipation, cultural self-reliance or political liberation, the desire for universal reason or for ethical reasons – all these must contribute to an international opposition if we want to succeed in creating a global solidarity against the power and control of special interests.

Only the development of an international opposition based on widely varying sources can achieve the influence necessary to neutralize today's powerful special interests – be they TNCs that want to pull the entire world into their process of commercialization; or corrupt members of the elite who sacrifice the futures of all to secure their power and wealth; multilateral institutions that organize and secure the system of maximum exploitation; or all the patriarchs who want to withhold complete and equal political, economic and cultural participation on the basis of self-determination from the female half of the world's population.

We are looking for alliances in the South, East and West.

Alliances in the South

The face of colonialism has changed. The military occupiers who secured the exploitative policies of the colonialists have been replaced by a neocolonial structure of trade policies that works to the disadvantage of the Third World but is politically supported by self-serving members of the elite and bureaucracies at the national and multilateral level. The most modern variant is financial neocolonialism, which uses high foreign debts to bind the economic structures of the developing countries to the interests of the North.

These new forms of repression have given birth to new forms of resistance and emancipation. There are few countries left where liberation movements must fight for political rights and the right to independence of the majority or broad sections of the population. Where this is still the case, our solidarity is still needed.

In the countries of the South, however, new social movements have become more important. With regional differences, a broad network of groups fighting for complete human and civil rights has developed. This network offers determined opposition to unconditional incorporation into the culturally and environmentally destructive capitalist structure.

Within this network are farmers' organizations seeking to secure regional food production with locally appropriate agricultural methods rather than produce cash crops for Western supermarkets; groups fighting the sacrifice of the environment to rapid world market integration; women's groups opposing male domination of all aspects of society and its possible expansion through economic measures for structural adjustment and profit-oriented population policies; civil and human rights' organizations that oppose internal colonialization; ethnic groups threatened by the loss of their natural and cultural environment and thereby their identity and existence; grassroots' church organizations whose theology of liberation is often opposed to a clergy allied with those in power; and trade unions that sue for employee rights in the industrial development centres.

The Greens consider the global networking of this opposition and the development of its international political influence to be a task of utmost urgency. Representative forces of these social groups and NGOs must be able to represent their interests within the framework of the United Nations.

We will also seek intensive co-operation with governments that base their policies on the interests of their people. However, even when there is tension between governmental policies and popular demands, a country may still have legitimate concerns on an international level that should be supported. Although in accordance with human rights' regulations we support oppositional groups, we cannot, in the effort to develop a global opposition, refuse to co-operate with nations whose governments we criticize.

The driving forces in the Third World that must be politically, economically and culturally emancipated are – despite their actual powerlessness – among the most important reasons for world economic relations based on solidarity. Their interests should not be allowed to be functionalized, but should instead be totally recognized as legitimate demands. In the Third World, even more so than in the West, ecological and social questions should not be played against each other. Environmental problems in the Third World can be solved only hand-in-hand with social problems.

In a policy of alliances based on mutual acceptance, alternative movements in Western industrialized countries must renounce their structural advantages to avoid a kind of 'alternative neo-colonialism'.

Unlike Western Europe, where the role of the individual nation is moving towards its historical end, the recent creation of independent nations in large regions of the Third World was an act of emancipation. The West must not encroach upon developing countries' national sovereignty, but their independence should not prevent joint opposition with progressives in industrialized countries. Discussions and negotiations must take place at an absolutely equal political level. This does not exclude difficult controversies. We want to replace unilateral conditions and deals with structurally stronger industrial countries with a round table where regional groups have equal footing and can present their mutual expectations. We oppose alternative 'blackmailing'. Democracy and ecological awareness must also come from the grassroots in the Third World, if they are to last.

Foreign debt of developing countries[1] ($bn.)

	1984	1985	1986	1987	1988[2]	1989[2]
Long-term debt	687	794	894	996	1020	1000
from open sources	238	305	364	437	450	460
from private sources	449	489	530	559	570	540
Short-term debt[3]	165	169	159	173	180	175
Other developing countries	81	89	99	111	120	125
Total	933	1051	1152	1281	1320	1300

[1]With the exception of the catagory other developing countries' and the total of 111;
[2]Provisional dates and estimates. [3]Inclusive of the international exchange currency.

Debt servicing

	1983	1984	1985	1986	1987	1988[5]
Indebtedness	645	687	794	894	997	1020
Gross capital influx	97	92	89	88	87	88
Repayments	45	49	56	62	71	72
Interest payments	47	53	56	55	54	59
Net capital influx	52	43	33	26	16	16
Net transfer of resources	5	-10	-23	-29	-38	-43

[4] Only on long-term debt. [5] Estimates

Source: *Neue Züricher Zeitung*

Green international trade policies that seek co-operation on an international level with states and their governments, but domestically with the opposition, must strictly distinguish between state and non-state levels. The support of local groups within a country by the Greens or a Green-controlled government, must be carried out by NGOs. Along with existing groups and organizations this also includes foundations which support 'green' principles.

To create a multipolar world, it is necessary to counter the trend towards subjugation of individual southern regions to the economic centres in the West. The United States is appropriating Latin America; Japan, South-East Asia; and the EC, Africa, although serious conflicts over these claims do take place.

On the contrary, we support the expansion of economic and political South-South co-operation and regional development.

Alliances in the East

After the fall of the old power structures, the battle over the best direction for future development in Eastern Europe began. Should an independent economic system be built beyond the boundaries of the centrally planned economy, willing to co-operate with other economic blocs? Or should there be a fusion with the West – basically the same as subordination to it? With a world economic order based on solidarity in mind, we hope that when the economies of the former Comecon countries purchase know-how and market techniques on the world market, they do not purchase its unscrupulousness as well.

In Eastern Europe the Greens will above all support those who, despite their bad experiences, continue to believe that the world economy should be based on solidarity and reason instead of money and power. This awareness goes right across the new party structures in the Eastern European states, and although stamped on and dragged through the mud, it remains part of the culture.

As these positive values were effectively used against the corruption of the old regimes, they may become the source of resistance against the unlimited introduction of a ruthless Western mentality. Solidarity – complemented by the awareness that has been lacking up to this point, that efficiency is indispensable in every economic system – could become a productive energy for humanely redesigning the economy. The Greens will look for dialogue with the representatives of this viewpoint to help develop their strength and defensive strategies against Western attempts at full incorporation of the East.

Nevertheless, even if other tendencies prevail, there will soon be organizations and social groups open to the ideas presented here. Complete acceptance of the Western capitalist model will lead to a new social order in Eastern societies. Many, who, at the beginning of this process, placed great personal hopes in a Western orientation and had faith in equal opportunity will be forced to discover that they must carry the burden for the emerging economy while its blessings pass them by. When the hoped-for consumption boom not only fails to appear, but additional economizing is required to serve Western capital investments, the early optimism will turn into even greater dismay. This will also be the case for people in the former GDR.

It is highly probable that social processes similar to those in deeply indebted Third World countries will take place in Eastern Europe. The future of newly experienced democracy under these conditions, whether it will be able to distribute the social burden fairly or will react repressively against the discontent, will depend on how much potential for solidarity remains.

Even when the East remains oriented towards the West, the Greens will support the forces of solidarity simply as a corrective measure. The Greens and all those with whom they co-operate closely will – in a unified Germany, too – need to show clearly that they are available for discussion and co-operation with the disillusioned, to prevent a violent form of protest.

Even before the revolutions in Eastern Europe, growing numbers of informal groups had taken up the cause of the seriously damaged environment. Feminist critique of the retention of paternalistic structures, despite improved professional opportunities, was also widely debated at the informal level. These informal groups provide a broad field of contacts for green politics.

The battle over the incorporation or independence of Eastern Europe will not be determined by an act of self-determination in eastern countries alone. The development of the Western balance of power will also be key. Our task is to block expansive and aggressive strategies. We must let the supporters of reform in the East know that during economic negotiations at the national level there are Western reformers who support them.

On the path towards reconstruction, the Eastern European economies must not enter into competition for resources with the countries in crisis in the South. East-West rapprochement must not be carried on the back of the South.

The West: a change of power and redirection

The most important areas for the Greens' political initiatives are in the OECD countries. A change of international relationships based on solidarity will not be possible without significant power changes in the dominant centres of the world economy. The political and economic structural adjustments required for this have been described by the Greens in their Programme for the Ecological and Social Reshaping of Industrial Society.

But new political ideas are only a frame to be filled with concrete concepts for redirecting economic processes. Complete economic control and private profit-making no longer coincide; the former is clearly in the service of the latter. Separating the two and strengthening the emphasis on ecological economics and fair distribution, to make the social and ecological reordering of the industrial system the social framework for a private economy and to expand private control over business processes via transfer of control rights to the personnel, will meet with strong opposition from current interests.

It is certainly worthwhile to seek a dialogue with today's business leaders over an immediate ecological restructuring. Such restructuring will hardly be possible without the technical management of people who will have to change their views. It is, however, unlikely that corporate strategists, whose only goal is capital growth, will be able to reorient their thinking. Dialogue alone will not be sufficient to persuade multinational corporations to renounce their power, which is a prerequisite for a world economy based on solidarity. Power must be won by building countervailing forces.

Every organization, institution and group is invited to join us in implementing a world economic order based on solidarity if they share the two basic premises that have motivated us. First, to seriously begin the long overdue ecological and social restructuring of our own industrial system, we cannot remain within national or European borders. Every national economic restructuring process requires reliable foreign trade safeguards. Secondly, if we are serious about solidarity with the poor and the poorest peoples of the world, we cannot continue to rely on classical economic development theory, but must insist that the legitimate interests of these people become the basis of the Western industrial powers' foreign trade policies.

The social movements and non-parliamentary groups that have fought for fundamental changes in economic policies and lifestyles, and the new groups opposed to the ruling development logic, must provide the necessary social force – transformed into political power – to bring about alternative international economic policies.

Environmental and social organizations, feminist groups and disarmament initiatives, the Third World solidarity movement and development organizations, farmer and consumer groups, foreign workers, refugees and ethnic minorities – we share their interests and goals. It is our responsibility to represent the foreign trade policy interests that these groups are usually unable to express successfully due to their limited political influence (see Glossary: BUKO).

The emancipation of women: Today's global economic structures are patriarchal, through and through. World politics is not only dominated by men, but men also perpetuate their superior position of power towards women by assigning them the unpaid work of reproduction. This does not only mean the dominant orientation of women towards housework, but also to their functionalization and exploitation by modern technologies such as gene or biological technology.

In some regions of the Third World, however, women's household subsistence work is the backbone of the economy and thus, exceptionally, also a source of female power. The often forced process of world market integration undermines this important social position, driving women into dependency on loans or even into prostitution, and forcing them into the Western model of the nuclear family, while their access to new techniques and methods of financing remains blocked.

Our foreign economic proposals not only take up important feminist demands, they also try to extend the idea of solidarity to the relationship between the sexes. A permanent, intensive discussion on alternative foreign trade policies and feminism could significantly increase the chances for both (see Chapter 2 and Appendix 1).

Trade unions: We also hope that trade unions will become our allies. Within unions there is growing awareness that unlimited world market-oriented growth not only creates room for higher wages, but also forces rationalization of production and thus leads to job losses and, because of the destruction of the natural environment, a reduction in the quality of life that workers expect. Increasing experience shows that aggressive Third World policies may benefit local employees in the short-term, but ultimately add to the corporation's room to manoeuvre and thereby undermine union opposition for some time.

Maintaining opportunities for union negotiations is connected to the mobility of a corporation; conversely, it is precisely the unions that will have to attempt to control the transnational activities of corporations via improvements in their own organization. They are predestined to international co-operation with representatives of related interests. The ecological and social restructuring of our economic system, for which the foreign trade aspect is being developed here, will only be achieved by activities of organized workers in and outside their workplaces (see Chapter 6).

Consumer organizations: More and more people are becoming aware of their power as consumers. Consumer organizations that were primarily concerned with quality-price comparisons are now increasingly incorporating ecological criteria into their product analysis and pointing out products associated with unjust world economic situations. Their educational work can contribute to greater questioning of the Western consumption model and the reorganization of private consumer needs with consideration of misdirected global ecological developments and injustices.

In a world economy based on solidarity, to continue present Western habits of consumption will be impossible. Thus political solidarity will have to extend to the private realm. The effects of attempts at consumer self-help, such as boycotts, could extend beyond consumer matters to become a possible form of action to draw attention to economic, political, ecological or social abuses, also in a global context, and to create pressure for change. An alternative foreign trade policy should welcome consumer organizations and critics of consumption as reinforcement for its own efforts and take the political initiative to improve the insecure legal position of concerned and aware consumers (see Glossary: IOCU).

Entrepreneurship: It will not be necessary to wait until employees have more power in corporate decision-making to find allies in the corporate sector. The entire alternative business sector is already aware of and open to a global redirection of development. Even some traditional entrepreneurs have come to understand that a company's interests are not necessarily those of society as a whole. These entrepreneurs attempt to incorporate a long-term adjustment of private market-oriented economics to global demands for North-South parity and natural resource protection into their investment and marketing decisions.

As it is impossible to do without private initiative, particularly from smaller and medium-sized companies, dialogue in this area is not only useful for Green economic policy, it is necessary. The conditions of work and participation in these businesses should, however, not be neglected despite possible co-operation in ecological areas. In the large corporations, critical shareholders are demanding ever more loudly that corporation policies be oriented towards more than the business goal of increased profits. These efforts must be supported, as they may be the seeds of far-reaching democratization of the corporate structure.

Foreign workers and refugees: Foreign workers and refugees from economically weak regions of the world have come in great numbers to the prosperous West. Most are not just interested in personal gain; they hope that things will improve for those back home. These emigrants, whose payments home have become a considerable factor in foreign trade, can expose us to the experience and knowledge of other cultures; they must not be discriminated against. Foreign workers and refugees are welcome partners, not only as fellow residents but also in common activities aimed at improving the situation in their home countries.

In the future we must make an effort to increase solidarity work with Third World countries and develop intensive relations to the world market-oriented modernization that is unfortunately taking place in the other OECD bloc countries.

Critical church groups: Ever more religious groups are demanding, often against the wishes of church authorities, that the social principles of Christianity become more than wishful thinking. Grassroots' church groups take up the admonitions of liberation theology not to misuse Christian values to legitimate unjust structures. Their ideas for restructuring the world on the basis of solidarity are progressive in a humanitarian sense and parallel those of the Greens, especially in the area of church development aid services and some official church positions. Anyone working for global justice and the protection of creation based on ethical convictions should be able to support our programme.

This programme puts the Greens in competition with the other German political parties. They have also begun to realize that global problems such as hunger, poverty and ecological disasters require counter strategies. In this context no party can fail to discuss the framework of the global economy. It must not, however, be overlooked that strategies are sometimes hidden that are absolutely counterproductive and incompatible. In principle, the liberals, conservatives and important sections of the social democrats expect to solve the problem with further deregulation of the market and liberalization of capital transactions, even if recently, they have to varying degrees become ready to cushion the negative social and environmental effects of these policies.

In our view they are declaring the cause of the problem to be the answer. Although with respect to individual issues co-operation is occasionally possible, we are still clearly opposed to these parties and tendencies. Nevertheless, in the German Social Democratic Party, in Green, Socialist and other left-oriented parties both in and out of Europe there are strong political tendencies with which co-operation could be considered and even seems to be worthwhile. Any Green participation in the national German government must also depend upon foreign economic policy similarities and differences.

Reforming institutions and the institutions of reform

We believe that the question of whether necessary political change can be achieved by public pressure or through institutional reform has been decided. Social forces and political power are contingent upon one another. The demands and pressure from the actions of social movements, organizations, groups and parties, first have an effect when they are transformed into institutional goals, and these goals become the official model for action.

In turn, institutional changes that are not simply superficial are made possible only through massive changes in articulated political consciousness. Green foreign economic policy will, therefore, not only try socially to strengthen groups that strive for a world economy based on solidarity, but will also try to help translate their activities into institutional reforms. While the primary task of each social action group remains development of the necessary political pressure, it is above all the task of the Green Party to dedicate ourselves to determining which institutional measures must be taken and to present these proposals to the government with corresponding public support.

Foreign trade responsibilities are increasingly transferred from the German federal government to European Community institutions. It is thus questionable even to talk about a German foreign economic policy. Through the Single European Act the EC will, as a single economic area, develop joint policies on relations with other blocs and regions. Furthermore, EC members have given up certain national rights to the EC, such as control over the freedom of establishment of businesses. We will thus have increasingly to address our demands to the EC Commission.

This body is, however, far from democratic. National parties and their parliamentary groups have practically no influence in Commission opinions or direct participation in passing regulations or decisions. Demands for a democratization of the EC can be found in the Greens' European Programme (see Chapter 5).

In the future, the Green/alternative parliamentary groups in the European Parliament will have increasingly to express ideas on a world economy based on solidarity. Despite the transfer of national sovereignty rights to a technocratic commission, European politics remains tied to the political will of the individual member nations. If the appropriate political will is there, the delegation of responsibilities to the EC level could be reversed. So we must continue to present our demands to the federal government. Its task is to adjust its foreign trade instruments to alternative goals, to win political acceptance within the EC for these new perspectives, and to present them in CSCE negotiations and discussions in the United Nations.

In our opinion the UN should become the most important level for action on world economic questions. The German federal government and the EC must be urged actively to implement human rights, as proclaimed by the UN, and also to urge other members to do so. This does not apply only to political human rights, often limited to civil rights; to establish a world economy based on solidarity, social human rights – including the right to economic development – are especially essential. Closely related to these are a series of internationally recognized regulations such as those of the International Labour Organization (ILO) or resolutions and codices that attempt to normalize individual aspects of economic relations.

The strongly centralized, over-bureaucratic and sluggish structure of the UN has been justifiably criticized. But this has not given the club of industrialized nations the right to determine the fate of the world economy according to their own desires while some 90 per cent of the world's countries remain excluded from this process.

The economic summit of the richest industrialized nations – falsely called the World Economic Summit – must be replaced by a formal commission within the framework of the UN in which all national groups participate. A world economic council meeting year round could assume this position. It could structurally secure the goal of just and ecological world trade policies and improve exchange relations for Third World nations. Analogous to the Security Council responsible for foreign policy issues, a World Economic Council could routinely control the observance of agreements ratified by its members (see Chapters 2, 3, 4).

The jurisdiction of the international courts must be meaningfully expanded where violations of economic policy agreements are concerned. As a centralized executive authority for implementing UN regulations is not desirable, codices and rulings derive their authority only from the voluntary commitment of EC members to obey the set guidelines. An element of national sovereignty must be relinquished to the higher level. At the same time all nations must guarantee the ratified regulations. A country that flagrantly violates the regulations and corresponding decisions of the court authorities must expect to be ostracized by the other nations. The introduction of obligatory codices and their strict supervision could become an important instrument for controlling transnational corporations.

The UNCTAD, as an institution particularly responsible for Third World interests, must be politically and financially strengthened (see Appendix 2). In addition to its new goals of resource protection and independent development, UNCTAD should be dedicated to North-South trade policies that are advantageous to developing countries. This means that beyond the administration of raw materials' funds, UNCTAD must protect development cartels, that is, defensive protectionism of structurally inferior nations. It must also place sanctions on aggressive protectionism and export expansionism of superior nations. UNCTAD could especially control trade in sensitive goods by placing them on so-called 'positive lists'. Dangerous goods could be completely banned from world trade.

The GATT must be institutionally developed and integrated into the UN framework. The basis of its work must be generally to determine and control the principles of trade based on solidarity and the positive discrimination of the so-called developing countries. UNCTAD and GATT would in this way become two windows in a new International Trade Organization.

The necessary restructuring of the UN special organizations, the International Monetary Fund (IMF) and the World Bank, has already been discussed in Chapter 4.

The German federal government should propose to the UN that it pass an international environment convention. The UN World Economic Council proposed by the Greens should also take on the function of a UN Ecological Council. This Council could be granted the authority to manage the environmental fund we propose. The overall goal of this Council would be the global realization of ecological economic policies.

Because, in the long-term, ecological and social reorientation of the world economy will be possible only through grassroots efforts in many societies, these societies should not be represented at the UN level by their governments alone. It must be possible, without offending principles of democratic representation, to create an advisory status for non-governmental organizations. This must be a key element in reform of the UN.

At the national level, social pressure must be generated to make it possible to replace the 'law on stability and growth' with a new basic economic law aimed at securing an economic structure compatible with social and environmental requirements. Instead of the current goal of an absolute balance in foreign trade, the aim could be a relative imbalance in favour of weaker partners through the requirement of self-imposed restraints, export restrictions and encouragement of imports. Ecological economic policies must be a major goal. Reporting requirements on the ecological costs of foreign trade, plans for toxic substance reduction and for reduction in the use of limited resources are particularly necessary.

In this context the tools of foreign trade must be reorganized. This includes legal instruments like Hermes export guarantees, investment protection and double taxation agreements as well as operative tools. For example, the bilateral chambers of trade and commerce should be instructed by political resolution to renounce their present goal of export maximization and to include church, trade union, development and consumer organizations in their activities.

Laws should require as much reporting on the activities of multinational corporations as possible, with the final goal of publicizing the need to break up these companies. Controls can be improved by the host country principle and the establishment of international anti-trust regulations. It is necessary for the German federal government to pass a bill as soon as possible to control the international activities of the large private banks. In this context the speculative aspects of financial and stock markets should also be dealt with.

The current federal Ministry for Economic Co-operation (BMZ) must be granted greater authority on the basis of the newly defined goals. At the very least, all the responsibilities that involved material and cultural North-South co-operation currently spread out among numerous ministries should be concentrated there. The areas of bilateral capital and technological aid, which for the most part benefit German foreign trade interests, must be thoroughly dismantled. Multilateral co-operation action with equal participation from recipient countries should be given preference over bilateral measures. International programme support should be given preference over national programmes. Financial and technological aid organizations can count on reduced government funding. The German Development Agency (DEG), which has arranged capital investments with overwhelmingly damaging effects, should be dissolved. The reduction in funding in the bilateral area should exclude non-governmental organizations.

Lifestyle and political campaigns

Changes in lifestyle . . .

Changes in global economic relations are not just questions of grassroots' political pressure and democratic reform. They also involve changes in perspective and private behaviour. If world trade is to be reduced, made more ecological and fairer for the populations of the Third World, then the West's private lifestyles must undergo major changes.

A debate over whether the boycott of certain consumer items will help the people of the South or whether, on the contrary, that solidarity with poorer populations will bring about reduced consumption as an unavoidable economic consequence, is useless. In either case, it will lead to shortages and price increases for products from the South. But changes in demand can influence the supply of goods and to a certain degree exchange relations and investment decisions. A basic requirement is knowing the problems associated with individual product lines, information that ecological consumer groups can contribute. A series of examples shows how changes in consumer behaviour can back up political demands for economic reordering:

* Boycotting tropical woods from primeval forests can support the ban on imports.
* Boycotts of hamburger fast-food chains can expose the relation between debt, export-oriented livestock raising, forest destruction and global warming.
* The boycott of South African products can support the UN embargo against this nation's apartheid.
* Purchasing products from Third World shops can support the direct marketing of products from progressively organized producers.

. . . and opposition

It will only be possible to establish a new economic world order and the institutions necessary for its implementation if the hoped for social alliances build their power through broad political campaigns. The type and extent of these campaigns cannot be formulated in a written programme. They depend on the internal decisions of the individual alliance members and the political situation. When the entire power of social and political groups subsides, the negotiating level of directed lobbying carried out by groups and organizations remains as a constant that, in turn, in times of high public political pressure can replenish its canon of concepts and demands.

The Greens see improving the exchange between the new social movements and older movements now organized as associations, plus the introduction of our own ideas, as important parts of our political work. As long as the opportunity exists to spread alternative ideas among the population through action campaigns, and thus pressure the administrators of the status quo, the Greens will make this the focus of our activities.

The past few years have provided us with a series of examples of how highly complex foreign trade topics can be focused on politically, through campaigns of various dimensions. Recent campaigns have addressed the following issues:

* ending weapons exports
* EC farm policy
* GATT and free trade
* the preservation of tropical forests
* actions by critical shareholders
* ending pesticide exports
* the 'World' Economic Summit
* against the policies of the International Monetary Fund and the World Bank; this was a comprehensive and systematic effort that introduced new approaches.

This international economic political programme is the result of these campaigns. The Greens will continue to support such efforts, and use their concepts and demands in the future development of our programme.

Appendix 1: Women of the South: feminization of the crisis

The globalization of capitalism has been analysed: countries of the South caught between indebtedness and structural adjustment; the East with its political upheavals and the exhaustion of the real socialist economic systems. However, where it concerns the appropriation of natural resources, of labour and – least visible – of unpaid women's work, the analysis falters.

An analysis excluding the hard work of women – every water-, firewood- and shopping-bag carrier, every universal diaper- and dish-washer, each life-long chopping, bargaining, cooking, and sweeping woman in the real utopia of a new world economic order – cannot speak of solidarity.

The shock absorber of structural adjustment

In the 1980s the 'feminization of poverty' was already a well-known expression. In recent years the debt débâcle and the drop in raw materials prices on the world market have once again had a profound effect on the survival conditions of many women in the South. To secure food, women are forced to increase cultivation and production of goods for individual use, that is, subsistence economics. At the same time, they need more money to satisfy their basic needs, therefore their integration into the market is necessary. As this conflict is seldom overcome with the sharing of work within the family, women attempt to solve the problem alone by working overtime.

The roles women are allotted in the debt drama are varied and flexible. They are supposed individually to share costs with the debt-plagued state and absorb the social hardships of devaluation, cancelling subsidies and social deterioration. National budget crises are increasingly being transferred to private households; women must make up for price increases with thriftiness, imagination and above all extra work. There is no money to buy food in larger and more economical quantities so women start to press oil themselves again, or make their own soap. To save energy they prepare only food with short cooking times. Bus fares are beyond their means, so once again they go by foot.

'Cost sharing' is the participatory sounding slogan that means school fees and the price of health services and medicine shoot up. Governments close kindergartens and medical facilities in rural areas, there are medication and school supply shortages, teachers and nurses wait months for their paychecks, little girls are the first to be kept home when school fees become too expensive.

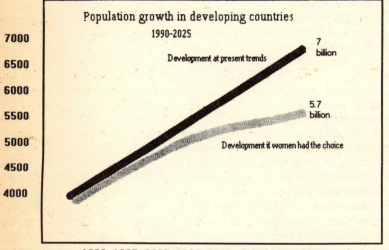

Source: Ken Hill, John Hopkins University, School of Hygiene and Public Health, using US and World Bank models.

Women's self-help groups formed in the daily struggle for existence are calculated in the structural adjustment by the development managers as 'social shock absorbers'. A World Bank study on Africa in the 1990s puts it concisely: 'Women and women's groups could furnish a considerable contribution to the improvement of social payments.' Self-help activities from the community kitchens in the barrios of Latin American cities to the savings co-operatives in rural African regions to the organization of grassroots' health services in Indian cities, projects that are collective, everyday management strategies still rooted in the 'moral economy', are simply functionalized to buffer social decline caused by government policy.

The area that the World Bank strategists allocate for the integration of women into the market and money economy is primarily the 'informal sector'. The majority of women organized into this sector survive with a patchwork of different occupations: mornings as house servant, afternoons working with out-patients, evenings as hairdresser for neighbours.

While economists propagate the 'informal' economy as existence security for a large number of poor people, the most intense exploitative and oppressive mechanisms predominate. Development aid offers women 'income generating' programmes and small credits for poultry, sewing machines or sales stands as vehicles for entering the market. The building and expansion of domestic processing and marketing is, however, crippled by the flood of cheap products (from second-hand clothing to EC agricultural products). Women rarely survive this competitive battle. They are often thrown back to activities that the state has criminalized for various reasons: prostitution, bootlegging, trade in contraband, and so on.

The marginal positions that women have occupied in formal areas of the economy are endangered by the cut-backs in state bureaucracies. Women in the lower positions in administration and health services are the first to be fired. They have little chance competing with men for the few positions in industry.

As foreign currency earnings are debtor countries' foremost economic policy goal, export-oriented enterprises and foreign investment are encouraged. Free trade zones, with profit earnings based on low wages for women's work, have become a model for an economic leap forward. Governments welcome every form of foreign currency earnings, from the export production of the small, women farmers' vegetables, flowers and nuts, craftswomen's embroidery, crochet work and baskets, through sex tourism, all the way to supplying female emigrant workers, house servants, prostitutes and mail-order wives.

Women and women's fertility are held responsible for the spread of poverty and environmental damage. In this case the correlation between poverty, low levels of education, reduced opportunity and high birth rates has been clearly proved. Yet aggressive family planning policies are offered as the solution. Means of birth control that are often health endangering and indifferent to the socio-cultural needs of women are offered, sometimes even forced, and an *ad hoc* change in perspective on motherhood is expected.

As in the West, the growing flexibility of paid and unpaid female workers in the South can be observed in new crisis situations. Women adjust to development requirements such as increased productivity and social decline. The 'resource' woman is being used more extensively and, according to the economic situation and development goals of greater priority, is moved about as a manoeuvrable mass between the subsistence and commodities economies.

Feminization of responsibility

In addition to the situation of women described above, the economic crisis is breaking up families. In many regions of Latin America, the Caribbean and Africa the number of woman-led households is growing. Whether the men leave in search of work in the city, on plantations or in mines or simply steal away from family responsibilities, it is – especially in poorer families – the women who care for the children and the old.

This erosion of familial bonds is accompanied by a loss in traditional morals and identity. Prostitution is growing with urbanization. Violence against women is increasing everywhere as men thereby try to compensate for their weakened social position.

Development aid participates in this growing polarization of the sexes with project support in the self-help area. Where grassroots' activities are supported, the cynicism of 'let the women do it' is widespread due to the impressive art of improvization and dependability shown by women. Where the sharing of never-ending dirty work is concerned, the state and men are relieved of the burden and the sex-specific distribution of work is re-established. This should not be confused with the emancipatory support of women.

In general, over the past decade the combined power of crises – economic, ecological, socio-cultural – has made women's development workers painfully aware of the powerlessness of women's projects. The purpose of aid programmes – received first in patriarchal mini-doses – is above all to act as repair shops for growth and world market development. If they relieve direct needs for the few, even the best cannot swing the rudder of development around.

Whereas women are forced to carry ever more of the burden and responsibility of development, they are not harvesting more of its fruits, either in terms of monetary or social rewards. During their daily struggle to survive, many women simply disappear from the focus on women that was present during the UN Decade of the Woman (1975 to 1985).

Women's organizations lack the time and power to fight against the systematic exclusion of women from property and inheritance rights and political power in general. The African Association of Women for Research and Development (AAWORD), a group of African women scientists, recently determined that there has been a political and legal roll-back in many nations that took a more liberal stance on women shortly after they became independent. The number of active women politicians is falling once again, rights are being cut-back, repression of women's organizations – as well as unions – is growing, fundamentalist currents with a conservative image of women are gaining influence in Islamic as well as Christian communities.

Towards fair development for women

A development model that is fair to women and includes different macro-economic structures and standards is necessary to dismantle the hierarchy of sex and stop overburdening women with work, responsibility and poverty and excluding them from access to means of production and political and controlling powers. The demand for the 'feminization of development' formulated as a result of the UN Decade of Women is based on the recognition that the development priorities set by women are grouped around the satisfaction of basic needs. These contradict the world market and growth-fixated development strategy that is based on the overexploitation of natural and human resources in the South.

The basis of development logic must be to overcome a number of functional exploitative dualisms. Conflicts between North and South, reproductive and productive activities, formal and informal sectors can no longer be viewed separately, but must be brought together, as with individual empowerment, regional sustainability and global solidarity. The approach and search for a form of development that is fair to women cannot be one-dimensional. Rather it is necessary that:

* in order to halt the increasing spread of poverty among the bulk of the population (mostly women), the transfer of resources and wealth from the South to the North in the form of unpaid raw materials, debt servicing and underpaid workers, in the free trade zones for example, be stopped. Debt elimination, the introduction of fair trade terms and appropriate wages must parallel campaigns to change consumer patterns. Women consumers in the North must learn that inexpensive coffee from Kenya, textiles from Sri Lanka and roses from Colombia are based on the poverty and exhaustion of women, and that these 'colonial' and luxury goods must cost more in a world future based on solidarity;

* policies and methods of production and consumption that protect the environment and natural resources must replace the careless exhaustion of natural resources for industrialization and the global supermarket, the unlimited consumption of raw materials and energy by the North, and the unscrupulous North-South 'damage' export (toxic waste, environmentally dangerous technologies and production) and atmospheric dumping (CFCs and CO_2 emissions).

Blaming women for the eco-crisis in the South is the same as blaming the victim for a crime. Poverty and shortages of cultivatable land due to deforestation and erosion caused by plantation farming force them to damage the environment during their search for firewood or through the use of non-ecological farming methods like fallow periods and the chopping down of biomass. Along with other development priorities, women's work that is focused on the satisfaction of basic needs – food cultivation for individual consumption, water and firewood gathering – must be supported and made easier, or alternative energy sources must be developed;

* work, knowledge and techniques be re-evaluated. The value of women's unpaid work, cultural knowledge and traditional technologies must be recognized instead of devalued or destroyed by the overvaluation of salaried jobs, modern knowledge and new technologies;

* countries and regions of the South have the chance to develop adequate agricultural self-sufficiency and production of consumer goods for the domestic market. Especially now with an eye on the 'European fortress' that will come with the single market in the European Community at the end of 1992;

* elements of the old 'moral economy' remain. The moral of mutual aid must

be strengthened despite the logic of profit maximization;

* debt elimination campaigns fundamentally change the traditional roles for women and men, and that acceptance of a new distribution of roles and work will be built (men in the kitchen! women in parliament!), so that future social rights and responsibilities, reproductive and productive work, as well as political decision-making power will be shared between the sexes;

* cultural and social diversity will be maintained and not repressed by the imposition of Western socio-cultural mores and the universalizing of the Judaeo-Christian nuclear family;

* instead of subsidies for financially intensive mega-projects or nutshell self-help projects, a more social form of structural change will be encouraged. There should be support for social movements, women's organizations and campaigns, participation and democratization processes, South-South co-operation, South-North contact, and public awareness campaigns especially in the North – all working against the catastrophic marginalization of the South to the benefit of the North.

Appendix 2: International agreement on raw materials

Raw materials are being discussed less and less by development policymakers and it is even rarer to hear of a raw materials policy. This is partly because the Third World movement has other priorities, as well as disillusionment over the result of so-called raw materials policy. The decreased importance of such policy in development discussions is understandable, but not acceptable. It is still the case that:

* the export of raw materials (not including oil) is responsible for more than 50 per cent of export earnings in 84 developing countries;
* twenty-three developing countries obtain 90 to 100 per cent of their export earnings with the export of lesser amounts of raw materials.

Clearly a large part of the Third World is still highly dependent upon the export of raw materials.

An integrated raw materials programme

In the 1970s the North-South dialogue broke down. The central demand of the Third World for a new world economic order was an integrated raw materials programme. This programme included proposals for agreements to stabilize the prices of 18 raw materials, and to finance such raw materials agreements it called for the establishment of a joint fund with two so-called 'windows', or financial sources.

* The first window would make US $4.5 billion available for the financing of buffer stocks to help stabilize prices through the purchase and sale of raw materials on the world market.
* The second window should make $1.5 billion available for investments in

raw materials processing facilities in the Third World or for the financing of new marketing techniques.

This integrated programme was the focus of the 1976 UN Conference on Trade and Development (UNCTAD) in Nairobi. Due to strong resistance from the industrial states the agreements achieved only the first steps in the direction of the programme. Agreement to establish a joint fund finally came in 1980, but it was a mini-edition of what was originally planned. The agreement provides for: $400 million for the first window; and $350 million for the second window.

In addition, the fund would not have a central steering function over the raw materials market, but rather would provide financial support for making agreements for individual raw materials and the work involved in carrying them out. But even the conditions required before the mini-fund comes into effect were only fulfilled at the 1987 UNCTAD conference in Geneva. At that time the Soviet Union joined the fund supporters, and other socialist countries followed. In this way the minimum financial contributions and number of member states specified in the agreement was finally achieved in 1988. Currently the contributing nations are discussing the concrete working methods of the joint fund.

Existing raw materials agreements

Although thus far official raw materials policies have not been realized within a comprehensive conceptual framework there are – and in some cases have been for a long time – raw materials agreements between producing and processing countries for seven raw materials: tin, cocoa, coffee, rubber, tropical wood, sugar and jute. For the most part, these agreements do not fulfil the demands of the Integrated Raw Materials Programme.

* Except for the coffee and cocoa agreements, the existing agreements use only the second window (the first window of the tin agreement is not currently in use), which merely provides for marketing and processing aid.
* Buffer stocks for stabilizing raw material prices are only provided for in the tin and cocoa agreements. The tin agreement has, however, expired, and the cocoa agreement was recently suspended until new agreements can be met by the member states.

Cocoa and coffee agreements
Fifty countries in the world produce cocoa, but 80 per cent of the world market is controlled by six of them: the Ivory Coast, Brazil, Malaysia, Ghana, Nigeria and Cameroon. The largest buyers and processors of cocoa are the EC and the US.

Against this background, most consumer and producer countries signed the cocoa agreement in 1972, the US alone refused to sign. In 1976, according to this agreement's guidelines, buffer stocks for cocoa were established to stabilize world cocoa prices. If the world market price exceeds the upper intervention price of the agreement, existing buffer stocks will be sold to bring about a price reduction. If the world market prices fall below the agreement's intervention price, then cocoa will be bought to stabilize prices via increased demand. The goal is to maintain a cocoa price within the upper and lower intervention price established in the agreement.

This buffer stock helped stabilize the price of cocoa until the mid-1980s. Since this time the buffer stock policy has constantly been on the verge of collapse. This is because the managers of the buffer stocks have experienced extreme financial difficulty in purchasing the large quantities of cocoa that are flooding the world market.

In 1988 the countries involved in the agreement produced 2.3 million tons of cocoa, but only 1.9 million tons were purchased. The buffer stocks had to purchase 400,000 surplus tons, bringing total surpluses to around one million tons. The management of the buffer stocks could not afford to finance cocoa storage at the standard price of one cent per ton. So the member states raised the required contribution to the buffer stock budget. The major producers, the Ivory Coast and Brazil, stopped paying the required contribution after the increase. As a result the cocoa agreement is verging on bankruptcy. New negotiations are underway, but the states involved have failed to reach an agreement on the financial question and the methods for supply reduction within the producer countries.

The Coffee Agreement has functioned somewhat better from the beginning. Negotiated within UNCTAD and in effect since 1963, it functions in a quite different way from the cocoa agreement.

The goal here was to maintain the price of coffee within a relatively wide margin. There are no buffer stocks of coffee; instead, price regulation is achieved with export quotas divided among the exporting countries. Depending upon how prices develop, a country may export more or less coffee. This regulation is not simple, as agreements on export quotas are difficult to reach, but this method does avoid the financial problems of buffer stocks.

The coffee agreement functioned very well until the mid-1980s. Since then, however, it has been in a state of crisis because the member states were only able to agree upon export quotas for short periods of time. The result is that since 1986 coffee prices have been falling, from 140 cents a pound in 1985 to 90 cents a pound at the end of 1987. This drop in price is distributed by the members of the coffee agreement, which includes practically all coffee consuming and producing countries, between winners and losers.

The losers are the producer countries, which experienced high export losses in 1987. In Latin America alone the drop in price has meant an estimated loss in earnings, calculated in US dollars, of about $800 million for Colombia; $400 million for Mexico; $200 million for El Salvador; $100 million for Costa Rica; $75 million for Guatemala; $50 million for Honduras; and $24 million for Nicaragua.

In general the exchange values for coffee exporting countries have dramatically worsened because of the drop in prices. In 1985 coffee producing countries needed to export 92 sacks of coffee to finance the purchase of one truck; in December 1989 this had risen to 332 sacks.

The winners of the drop in price were coffee consumers. A four-person blue-collar family in West Germany drank an average of 1,162 grams of roasted coffee per month in 1988. At the same level of consumption in 1989 this family saved 103 DM over 1985 prices.

The coffee agreement is currently suspended, but it is worthwhile examining why it functioned better than other raw materials agreements, such as those for cocoa or tin, for example.

There are several reasons for this. The demand for coffee has risen continuously over the past years. The system of export quotas proved to be considerably more successful than buffer stocks, partly because there is less incentive to overproduce continuously – and thereby less danger of a parallel market which gets around the attempts of the buffer stock management to stabilize prices. In addition, buffer stocks require high financial investment. But the system of export quotas is not without its problems. It makes the entrance of new producers to the market difficult, and functions only with a high degree of discipline among the producer countries. The high participation level in the coffee agreement was decisive to its success. Membership consists of the countries which account for 90 per cent of the export and 90 per cent of the import of coffee.

Prerequisites for successful raw materials agreements

From these different but in retrospect similarly disillusioning experiences with raw materials agreements the prerequisites for successful agreements can be determined:

* A high percentage of consumer and producer countries must participate in the raw materials agreement.

* As a price stabilizing mechanism export quotas – which require great discipline from participating countries – are more efficient than buffer stocks, which can only function with sufficient financing and large capacity.

* The price range between upper and lower intervention prices must to a certain extent be determined by market mechanisms. A stabilization price that is over the real market price for too long can endanger any raw materials agreement in the long term.

* Member states must subject themselves to the discipline of the raw materials agreement. They must not allow a parallel market to arise that circumvents the agreement's price stabilizing mechanism.

* Increasing demand for the corresponding raw material is a great advantage.

A look at these prerequisites for a successful raw materials agreement can easily lead to cynicism. The raw materials prices could not be stabilized in the past. According to UNCTAD reports, the prices of the 18 raw materials in the IRP of 1987 represent the buying capability that existed in 1938. The HWWA Institute for Economic Research in Hamburg reports that in 1986 the world market prices for raw materials were actually 30 per cent lower than their real value in 1980.

This development in raw materials prices shows that the prerequisites for a successful raw materials agreement have not been fulfilled – and not only this. It also shows that the framework for raw materials trading on the supply-side as well as the demand-side has changed drastically in the past decades. Only if this changed framework is taken into account can the present difficulties in reaching new raw materials agreements be understood or can the necessity of repeatedly introducing price stabilizing measures be eliminated.

On the supply-side, the following factors interfere with price stabilizing measures and result in sinking prices. Many producer countries are pushed into a disastrous vicious circle by the pressure of high foreign debts, which require large amounts of foreign currency for interest payments. Thus many highly indebted raw materials exporting countries increase their export of raw materials at all costs – even those of the environment and of raw materials prices themselves. Because the resultant surplus of raw materials is met by only a slight growth in demand, prices are forced down.

Transnational corporations dominate raw materials trading and attempt to get around agreements that they have been unable to prevent being ratified. For example, transnational companies moved tea production from Sri Lanka to Kenya because Kenya always refused to accept the export quota regulations of various agreements.

Problems in the demand-side arise largely from the fact that industrial states' increase in demand for raw materials is below average with respect to their own economic growth. There are many reasons for this. The structural changes in process benefit industries that use fewer raw materials more than those requiring high raw material input – computer chips have overtaken steel production.

The new technologies make it possible to achieve the same result with fewer raw materials (the tin layers of tinplate cans are increasingly thinner). Substitute materials are being increasingly developed. Plastics have replaced metals in many areas, as in the motor vehicle industry. Ecological awareness supports resource recycling, which means additional reduction in demand for raw materials. And demand for food products is stagnant because of increasing market saturation.

Under these conditions the chances for fulfilling the prerequisites for new raw materials agreements in the coming years do not look good. In addition, the discrediting of the planned economy also discredits mechanisms for stabilizing raw materials prices, as they also represent interference in the market process.

On-going need for raw materials policies

In the face of so many obstacles, hopes for future raw materials policy depend on two things. The joint fund began its work in the beginning of the 1990s. Although this will consist of only 'mini-payments' when compared with original plans, more capital will then be available for price stabilizing measures and for the second windows of raw materials agreements.

The debt crisis will be increasingly costly to the so-called First World – both ecologically and economically – because the Third World's high foreign debts force them to cut their rainforests for export, but at the same time prevent them from importing more from industrial states. The developing countries could try to bring in raw materials policy as a bargaining chip in strategies for solving the debt crisis.

In any case, the Third World needs a revised concept for the stabilization of raw materials prices which should be founded on the following main points:

* The stabilization of raw materials prices within a certain price range, to account somewhat for shifts in market prices. If stabilization prices are consistently above market prices, raw materials agreements will fail.

* It appears to make sense to avoid buffer stocks as a method of price stabilization. An alternative is the control of supply via export quotas – this saves money on storage and over-production, but requires discipline of the participating states.

* Regulations must be included in raw materials agreements that require consumer countries to apply protectionist measures against raw material shipments from countries not party to the raw materials agreement. This is the only way to prevent development of a parallel market and force all producer countries to participate in the agreement.

* The second window of raw materials agreements must finance measures for the processing of raw materials in developing countries and, if necessary, also measures for switching over production if consistent surpluses dominate the raw materials market.

The change in the framework of the supply and demand sides of the world market for raw materials and the 'triumph of capitalism' currently make the necessary steps for a new offensive in raw materials policy difficult. Given the unchanged, extreme importance of raw materials exports to developing countries, however, this offensive is more urgent than ever.

As the developing countries currently have little influence in controlling global policy they are dependent upon the solidarity of the Third World movement in the industrial states, and must hope that these groups do not forget raw materials policies in the pursuit of other priorities. Many developing countries' economic development is closely bound to the situation on the international raw materials market – stable and higher raw materials prices are at the core of an ecologically oriented global economic policy based on solidarity.

Appendix 3: Foreign trade in agricultural production in a world economic order based on solidarity

The catastrophic nutritional situation in many Third World countries reveals the basic inhumanity of the current world system of agricultural trade. While there has never been as much food produced in the world on a per capita basis as there is today, a growing number of people go hungry or suffer from malnutrition.

In the 1960s only around 2,300 k/cals were available per person daily, based on the sum of all agricultural goods produced per person. Today, with 1.8 billion more people on earth, some 2,600 k/cals are theoretically available to everyone daily. World agriculture can produce much more food than is necessary for the world population's nutritional needs, yet one person in ten goes hungry.

In the prevailing system of world agricultural trade, agricultural growth and the increasing integration of farmers and consumers into the 'global supermarket' goes alongside ever greater imbalances in the distribution of what is produced. It is increasingly the case that agricultural trade's 'rules of the game' and the principles of international competition determine the direction of agricultural development both in developing and industrial countries. Since the 1950s international trade in farm produce has grown twice as fast as agricultural production itself. Today 12 per cent of the world's agricultural goods are produced for the international market.

The world agricultural market has long been more than just a 'residual market' for the occasional sale of farm surpluses. Supplying world markets and opening up new markets in third countries, and thus increasing the international competitiveness of one's own agricultural sector, have become the leading premises of farm policy in the European Community and the United States.

In recent years there has been a dramatic shift in roles in world agricultural trade. Today, the industrial countries not only dominate industrial and service trade but, with the exception of Japan, they have also become the world's biggest food exporters. Until a few years ago the EC was still importing such foodstuffs as sugar and grains, but has since quickly developed into the most powerful agricultural exporter, along with the USA.

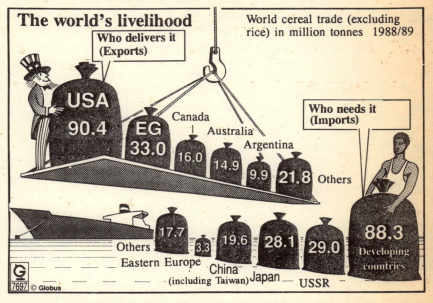

The world's livelihood

World cereal trade (excluding rice) in million tonnes 1988/89

Who delivers it (Exports)

USA 90.4

EG 33.0

Canada 16.0

Australia 14.9

9.9

Argentina 21.8

Others

Who needs it (Imports)

Others 17.7

Eastern Europe

3.3

China (including Taiwan)

19.6

Japan

28.1

USSR

29.0

88.3 Developing countries

7697 © Globus

The success of the European Community's agricultural sector on the world market is not primarily the result of an efficient agricultural sector, rather due to the purchasing power of EC taxpayers. At present, one-third of the total EC farm budget – an amount extending into the billions – is spent each year to subsidize European agribusiness exports that would otherwise not be saleable on the world market.

The disastrous results of this policy can be seen in the developing countries. Every year they lose market shares of world agricultural exports to the Western industrial countries. Despite the increasing economic marginalization of the sub-Saharan African countries in particular, their economies nevertheless continue to be seriously dependent on exports and thus on world market developments. The collapse in commodity prices in recent years has had a strong impact on the more than 50 developing countries that export mainly unprocessed raw materials and farm produce. The drop in value of agricultural exports from developing countries has caused losses of approximately $300 billion over the last 15 years – and profits for the importers benefiting from the low coffee, soya and tapioca prices.

The price decline on the world agricultural market is a direct consequence of EC and US export offensives. Their highly subsidized export battles have pushed prices for individual products down below production costs. Their export 'dumping' distorts local agriculture in many food-importing developing countries and forces small domestic producers out of the market. Independent food security in developing countries is being systematically undermined by subsidized farm products from the North, with the goal of making these countries dependent on food imports

The European farm sector's continuing dependence on highly subsidized agricultural raw materials is the flip side of the European Community's export success. The EC, which carries on two-thirds of its foreign agricultural trade with developing countries, continues to be the world's largest food importer. Its main imports are oil seed, grain substitutes and the tropical luxuries – tea, coffee, tobacco. It exports processed foods, and often meat and milk products, instant coffee or chocolate to the very countries that provided the necessary raw materials. Given the escalating tariff rates in the EC, there is almost no chance for Third World food-processing firms to sell their products in the EC with higher value added shares.

EC surpluses crowding world agricultural markets are harvests rooted in hunger. The production of agricultural raw materials for the European market not only occupies valuable farmland in the developing countries but is changing the form of agriculture there. Small producers and subsistence farming are forced out as commercial international production increases.

The world market's share in agribusiness (%)

	Exports		Imports	
	1967	1987	1967	1987
USA	14.4	12.3	11.5	10.5
France	4.3	8.1	5.6	6.5
Netherlands	4.3	7.4	3.2	4.5
Canada	5.4	5.8	2.1	2.0
W. Germany	1.9	5.5	9.5	10.3
UK	2.3	3.5	12.2	6.8
Belgium-Lux.	1.6	3.1	2.7	3.4
Australia	4.4	3.0		
Italy	2.1	2.8	5.9	7.4
Denmark	2.4	2.7	1.0	1.2
Japan			7.9	10.9
USSR	1.0	1.8	3.5	5.4
Spain	1.3	2.1	1.7	2.3
Total	45.4	58.1	66.8	71.2

Source: International Trade 1987/88, GATT secretariat, Genf 1988

Note: The community of the twelve in 1987 took a 37.7% share of the world's agrarian exports & 44.5% of imports.

The fertile land used in the Third World to grow feed for Western European pigs and cattle is estimated to be two to three times greater than West Germany's entire agricultural acreage. In African nations that have suffered repeated famine in recent years, an average of almost one-eighth of all arable soil is reserved for export production of coffee, tea, cocoa, bananas, and suchlike. Even in countries where agricultural export production takes up a small share of fertile soils, limited resources of water, agricultural credits, and so on go mainly to the export sector and thus fail to create opportunities for domestically oriented agriculture.

The dominant role of EC agricultural economics in the unequal division of agricultural labour is reflected in West Germany's foreign agricultural trade. West German farmers and consumers are especially connected to world trade. As one of the wealthiest nations, West Germany has the highest levels of agricultural imports per capita in the world. At the same time, West Germany is the fourth largest exporter of agricultural goods, including EC exports; some 20 per cent of West German agricultural production is exported. The food business comes before iron and steel as one of the most important export sectors in the West German economy.

Integration of West German agriculture into the international division of labour system is not without its consequences for German society. The structural change from single-family farms to agro-industrial, environmentally unsound production methods that involve ever more capital, accelerates with increased internationalization. The export successes of West Germany's farm industry do not help stabilize agricultural income; instead, they accelerate the demise of small farms.

Cheap imported animal feed allows large-scale livestock raising independent of available grazing land. Animals are increasingly raised in mass-production enclosed pens. Fully 80 per cent of the European Community's pork comes from the so-called 'pig belt', an area within a 200 km radius of Rotterdam's harbour. With the enormous expansion of markets, small producers are increasingly degraded into powerless raw materials suppliers for multinational agribusiness. They are increasingly played against each other as competitors, the more the food industry, dairies and meat mail-order houses switch over to raw materials from the greater EC region and beyond. The 'polypoly' of small agricultural producers is helpless against the oligopoly of the internationally interwoven agricultural industry.

The growing distance between producers and consumers also means longer transport routes and more processing. These cause enormous environmental destruction and waste resources. In OECD countries nearly one-fifth of the overall energy used is consumed by agriculture, from the production of fertilizer to food processing. Almost as much energy is used to transport and distribute foodstuffs as is required for their production. Concentrated agricultural production – from which the West German farmers earn 80 per cent of their income – is a result of inexpensive feed shipments. This is especially fatal from an ecological perspective. It takes, for example, approximately 20 times more energy to produce a kilogram of beef than the same amount of corn.

Already one-quarter of the world's population consumes around three-quarters of the world's resources. A further increase in energy waste by European agribusiness from the industrialization and internationalization of foodstuff production is ecologically irresponsible and goes hand in hand with the aggressive exploitation of resources from all corners of the world.

For consumers, the advantage of the expanding variety of goods available from global agricultural trade is only superficial. With the increasing distance between producers and consumers it becomes ever more difficult to get information on a product's origin and conditions, or the amount of processing and mode of transport involved. The agricultural products must be adjusted to the demands of industrial processing and long-distance shipping. Thus we have questionable preserving methods, such as irradiation or the cultivation of square tomatoes that are tasteless but easily packed, stacked and canned.

The international harmonization of food-related laws, indispensable for a 'global supermarket', will lead to a common denominator below the best available food-related and ecological standards, be it purity standards for milk products or bans on throw-away bottles. Natural foods do not easily adapt to the conditions of intra-regional trade – and the overall quality of our foods deteriorates under the imperative of extensive transportation and processing.

GATT's magic formula for a free global agricultural market

The various aspects of the current world agricultural crisis presented here are more or less connected to the structure of the global economic division of labour and the growth of international agricultural trade within the context of dominant trade structures. A reordering of world trade in agricultural products is urgently needed. Above all, EC foreign agricultural trade must be fundamentally restructured, as the EC is, to a large degree, responsible for current world market conditions that threaten Third World agricultural development and food supply.

The proposals for overcoming the agricultural trade crisis that are at present being discussed in the context of the GATT (General Agreements on Tariffs and Trade) negotiations are headed down a blind alley. GATT formulates internationally binding guidelines for the trade policies of more than 100 nations that have signed the agreement or apply its regulations. The treaty is thus one of the main pillars of the current world economic order. So far, GATT has applied a number of special rules to trade in farm produce, exempting agricultural trade from the basic requirements of a liberal and non-discriminatory trade policy. Article XI.2 of GATT allows for the establishment and maintenance of non-tariff barriers to trade (like quotas) in the agricultural sector. Article XX allows import restrictions to protect the life and the health of humans, animals and plants. Article XVI permits domestic and export agricultural subsidies.

So far the US-led liberalization effort has not been backed by the EC Commission, but is supported by Western European industrial groups. Its aim is to subject trade in agricultural produce, without exception, to the GATT principle of liberalization. This would prohibit import and export restrictions as well as production-related support programmes in the domestic agricultural

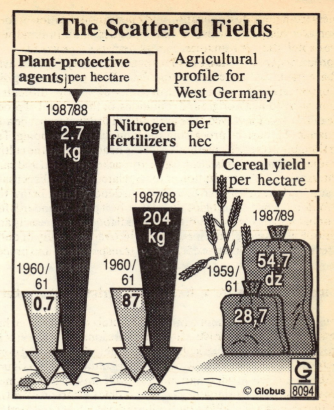

The Scattered Fields

Plant-protective agents per hectare

Agricultural profile for West Germany

1987/88
2.7 kg

Nitrogen fertilizers per hec

Cereal yield per hectare

1987/88
204 kg

1987/89
54.7 dz

1960/61
0.7

1960/61
87

1959/61
28.7

© Globus
8094

sector, eliminate supply and price controls in agricultural production, and stop export subsidies. In addition, free-trade apologists want the worldwide 'harmonization' of health and phytosanitary (plant health) regulations, and ultimately the harmonization of all food-related legislation. Their goal is to simplify and stimulate the international exchange of farm goods.

In this context legitimate consumer protection interests are discredited as 'trade barriers'. The GATT signatories have already agreed to abolish future standards, for food product laws determined by unelected and non-accountable bureaucrats. The demands for liberalization peak with the US government's cynical demands that future restrictions or bans on exports of foodstuffs to the integrated market no longer be allowed at all, even in the case of food shortages.

The full deregulation of national and international farm markets is supposed to create a breakthrough for international competition in agriculture in a government-free environment. But since the GATT only regulates government trade policies and not the activities of the private sector, the demand for a liberalization of agricultural markets in the context of GATT is tantamount to banning politically motivated limits on the profit maximizing of multinational agribusiness.

We must take into account the fact that, usually, private companies, not governments, are the active forces in agricultural trade, and only a dozen or so major agribusiness corporations transact most of the world's trade. Thus it is clear that allowing the 'free market' to take full control of agricultural development means leaving food production and food security up to corporate price agreements, the formation of cartels and the investment decisions of multinational agribusiness.

A world system based on solidarity

Liberalization of trade in agricultural produce runs counter to our vision of a world economic system based on solidarity. The primacy of er economy is only possible if the sovereignty of democratically legitimated authorities is guaranteed in trade and economic decision-making. Agriculture and food security are fundamentally important for all societies. Every country should have the right to sovereign decision-making, in agreement with all trading partners who may be affected, over the promotion and protection of agricultural development, environmental and consumer protection. Of course government sovereignty is a necessary condition for the primacy of policy over economy to be effective, but it is not in itself sufficient.

The GATT must guarantee respect for the measures countries take to protect their agricultural production against cheap farm imports, to guarantee food supplies, promote agricultural development in disadvantaged regions, control supply and prices on internal agricultural markets, and protect their environment and consumers. To the extent that these measures are not detrimental to the food security and welfare of other countries, they should be exempted from the catalogue of 'trade barriers' as defined by GATT.

The prerequisite for a world system of ecological agricultural trade based on solidarity is the democratic control of economic processes. Agricultural development must not be left to the steering function of the market – in other words, competition and lowest-cost production methods. Agricultural trade must instead be guided by principles of justice, preservation of natural resources, maintenance of regional economic and social independence, and the assurance of sufficient supplies of wholesome food.

Without the regulation of national and international markets, as well as minimum social and ecological standards in the spectrum of political objectives, it will not be possible to realize a global economic system of this kind. Today the range and extent of economic processes in the agricultural sector has long since undermined the ability of democratic authorities to exert control. There are two conclusions that can be drawn from this, each of which should be pursued: 1) there is a need to strengthen supranational regulatory mechanisms; and 2) a need to reduce the scope of economic policy decisions to a range that allows for democratic economic controls.

There is currently no international institution that could be a forum for ordering and controlling an ecological world agricultural trade based on solidarity. The International Trade Organization that was planned shortly after World War II under the auspices of the UN would have had this authority. But the ITO was not founded, and only the GATT remains as a political fragment of its potential tariff instruments. The original regulations on international cartel and competition laws, over resources and the support of 'less developed treaty members'' economic development contained in the ITO statutes, never found their way into the GATT.

Given its history and basic liberal outlook, the GATT could probably never be the forum for negotiating a global trade system based on solidarity. It will, however, be necessary in the GATT context to establish at least the basis for international cartel and competition laws, codes for technology transfer, as well as needed price and quota-regulating agreements on commodities. Similarly, the protective provisions of Article XX will have to be strengthened to create the prerequisites under international law for a global system of ecological agricultural trade based on solidarity.

A basic condition for establishing a new order of world trade is ending the governmental monopoly on representation in international committees and agreements such as the GATT, IMF or UNCTAD. The oppositional power of social movements can be effective only when they are included in decision-making processes on the international level (see Chapter 7).

We are strongly against the basic GATT ideology that a progressive integration of regions into the world market and growth of international trade will benefit all the trading partners involved. Given the wide variety and differences in production-related and ecological conditions in agricultural regions, sharpened international competition in the agricultural sector will result in economic and social misery as well as the ecological destruction of disadvantaged regions.

Viewed from the standpoint of balanced regional development, food security and the preservation of ecologically appropriate crops, agricultural production must be maintained in areas that are not competitive in world market terms. Thus we argue in favour of economic and trade-related regionalization of the agricultural sector. We also support establishing latitude for bilateral trade agreements that take into account individual social needs. We reject global strategies that – in the context of ruthless international competition guided by the imperative of a multilateral global trade system – fail to draw distinctions between the different needs of the world's various regions and societies.

Resistance to deregulation of agricultural markets must not be confused with support for prevailing European Community farm policy. EC agricultural protectionism is aggressive. By promoting an internationally competitive agribusiness and subsidizing exports, its objective is less one of protecting small farmers than of cornering agricultural markets.

Given the disastrous results of price reductions for Third World agricultural exports, the 'liberal' demands for a ban on all export subsidies should be supported without restraint. This ban should be extended to include private export dumping. There should be government restriction of cheap agricultural imports that threaten vigorous local and regional agricultural development.

Based on the principles presented here for an international socially and ecologically appropriate agricultural trade policy, we advocate:

* the legitimacy of trade-restricting measures that provide for environmental and consumer protection, food security and agricultural development in disadvantaged regions;

* elimination of export subsidies for farm products;

* unconditional recognition of protective UN conventions, such as the UN Declaration on Human Rights, the Convention on International Trade in Endangered Species of Wild Fauna and Flora, and the Worker Protection Convention of the ILO in GATT;

* bilateral trade policy agreements with developing countries granting improved market access in the framework of selective trade promotion efforts and preferences graduated in accordance with social needs;

* limitation of food aid in disaster situations. Food aid shipments should not come from EC surpluses, but rather 'triangular measures' should be taken, using surpluses within the disaster region;

* maintenance of a margin of preference for the poorest countries (LLDCs) for agricultural products (especially sugar and bananas) within the framework of lifting national bilateral trade quotas in the EC internal market;

* establishment of agreements on commodities that would regulate minimum and maximum prices as well as supply and purchase quotas for agricultural produce;

* the introduction and maintenance of high food-related standards, such as bans on the irradiation of foodstuffs and genetic manipulation of crop plants and farm animals;

* a body of international law on cartels and competition.

Appendix 4: The international illegal drug trade

International trade in illegal drugs is currently an important sector of the world economy. According to Interpol, US $500 billion are spent on drugs every year; the UN estimate is lower, some $300 billion. This amounts to approximately nine per cent of the volume of world trade, putting the drug trade second only to the weapons trade in volume, still higher than the oil trade. Illegal drug sales are as great as the total sales of all legal drugs – including alcohol, tobacco and pharmaceuticals!

A full one-third of these sales come from one country – the USA. But because of the present glut in the drug market, especially for cocaine, as well as the subsequent drop in excessive black market prices, an intensified 'development' of the European market is feared.

The estimated yearly revenues from illegal drug trading amount to $100 billion, promising profitable rates of return for this business. As these profits are invested in legal sectors of the local economy, in drug cultivation, and in the Western consumer countries, the political influence of the criminal investors grows along with their economic power.

Legal or illegal?

As with the weapons business, the drug trade vividly shows that a clear line cannot be drawn between the supposed exact opposites of 'organized crime' and 'professional white-collar management'.

Some of the addictive substances legal in Western countries today – such as alcohol, have on occasion been banned in the twentieth century, before prohibition was replaced by a taxation model. On the other hand, many of the drugs that are currently illegal in Western countries were sold legally and successfully right up to the twentieth century. The German pharmaceutical corporation Merck, for example, produced morphine for over a century for international sale, and cocaine and cannabis tinctures for more than 60 years.

The firm still holds the patent for 'Ecstasy'. The Bayer Corporation lauded the substance its chemists developed to treat morphium addicts – heroin.

Similar developments have taken place at the international level historically. For instance in two 'opium wars' merchants of the British East India Company, with the help of British war ships, forced opium exports on China despite the Chinese government's ban on the drug.

It can be concluded that as the classification of different drugs changed, a legal or illegal drug industry 'based on the division of labour' took over drug production and sales. In the meantime, the suppliers of both 'branches' have developed into transnational corporations due to the increased demand for drugsof all types.

The blurred boundary between the legal and illegal drug industries becomes even more obvious when their co-operation in today's production processes is observed. Special equipment and a series of basic (and legal) chemical materials are needed to produce such illegal drugs as heroin and cocaine; basic knowledge of chemistry is, of course, also required. According to investigative research, the latter is often provided for the drug producers in the industrial states or by the pharmaceutical corporations. Production equipment mostly comes from the United States.

The base chemicals (including ether, aceton, acetic acid-anhydrid) are supplied quite officially by large corporations in Brazil, China, the Netherlands and West Germany. Despite years of concrete evidence, such as that supplied by the US Drug Enforcement Agency (DEA), of extensive shipments by the West German firms Hoechst and Bayer, the German federal government regularly declares that they have 'no substantial findings' of any possible criminal activity. The new UN convention against drugs and the proposal for its implementation presented by the German government, which would introduce reporting requirements and sanctions for such exports, still does not include the most important substances.

The Green Party in Germany has therefore called for comprehensive monitoring of exports, especially to 'previously convicted' drug producer countries as well as effective sanctions in the case of violations.

Drug producing countries

Hardly any naturally occurring illegal drugs are cultivated in the Western consumer countries. By contrast, in the producer countries, there is either no demand or no criminalized demand for these substances. These drugs are produced and refined for export, or consumed locally as traditional medicinal or cultural plants (for example, coca leaves in Peru, cannabis in North Africa or Jamaica). This, incidentally, is one reason why there is heavy resistance to Western attempts to stop (or destroy with herbicides) the entire production of these substances, including that for domestic use.

Of the well-known producer countries, only the cocaine producing countries of Latin America – mainly Peru, Bolivia and Colombia – will be examined here. The effects of the drug trade in these countries on the bordering states of the region, such as Ecuador (transit and port facilities), Uruguay (money laundering), Mexico (transit) and Brazil (investments, retreat for major dealers), can be only briefly mentioned.

Building on the traditional importance and farming of the coca bush, especially in Peru and Bolivia, areas under cultivation have been continually expanded (in Bolivia for example to 70,000 hectares or 173,000 acres) to meet rising demand, from the USA for instance. Currently, Bolivia and Peru supply mainly the half-finished product, coca paste, to Colombia where – organized by the drug cartels – it is further processed and sold abroad.

The trusted form of economic relations, a 'division of labour' well known in North-South relations, is reproduced in these countries. Nonetheless, the workers who grow coca or produce coca paste are offered higher wages than for most jobs. The parallel drop in world market prices for precious metals from these countries is a further reason why so many farmers have become involved in coca production.

In addition, a large amount of the profits are reinvested in these countries, bringing real improvements in infrastructure. The social and political influence of the cartels in Colombia and of the guerrillas in Peru grew because they organized and directed this process and guaranteed their work force protection from government and foreign attempts at repression (such as the deployment of domestic or US soldiers). In this process the beginnings of autonomous structures have been created that fill the power vacuum in remote rural areas, a vacuum largely due to ineffective and in part corrupt government organization.

The profits from drug transactions are increasingly invested in legal economic areas in these countries, boosting the building industry or stock farming in Colombia, for example. Drug profits are greater than legal government foreign currency receipts. Characteristic of the situation is the famous offer of the drug baron Carlos Lehder to pay off Colombia's entire foreign debt if the government agreed not to subject him to criminal prosecution and extradition to the US.

The attempts of consumer countries to solve 'their' drug problem by stopping the supply from producer countries is doomed to failure. Repressive or even direct military aid or intervention, especially from the USA, is obviously not only directed at drugs, but also at the political opposition in these countries, for instance the guerrillas in Peru or Bolivia. Incentives to switch to other agricultural products cannot succeed as long as persistent drops in world market prices continue and stable purchase prices and better terms of trade are not guaranteed. Therefore, drug exports from the producing countries will continue to be an example of how competitive advantages between supply and demand in North-South trade relations can in one case make a 180 degree turn.

We see a way out only by decriminalization of drug use in the consumer countries, with government or state licensed drug distribution to regulate the supply from the producer countries and quantity and price agreements between state trading enterprises or licensed persons on both sides. Something of a utopia!

The consumer countries

The persistent criminalization of the use of certain drugs in most Western consumer countries guarantees a high black market price and thereby high profits for the drug cartels in the producer countries, the distributors and small dealers in the consumer countries.

The demand can apparently not be reduced, because the social costs of Western economic and social structures are inseparably related to increased rates of psychological disturbance and drug addiction. Adequate therapy and preventive measures are not being made available. Instead, there is a focus on criminal prosecution, not just against dealers to contain the availability of drugs, but also against individual consumers. Because of the existing organizational structure and police rights to search, the focus of activity is concentrated here, despite claims to the contrary. The punitive rather than curative approach drives the user – especially those on hard drugs like heroin – to finance their addiction through dealing, prostitution and criminal activities.

According to realistic estimates, the roughly 100,000 addicted hard drug users in West Germany need around 2,500 DM monthly to support their habits, a total of 7.3 billion DM per year. Given that stolen goods are sold by thieves for only ten to 20 per cent of their value, a sum five to ten times this amount must be stolen or somehow acquired. Experts estimate that two-thirds of all thefts in West Germany are drug related. A 1988 US government study estimated the total cost of illegal drug consumption at $60 billion a year. This problem, only touched upon here, is a serious economic aspect of illegal drug use.

Drug policy, not drug war

It is hardly surprising that there is discussion about the legal possibilities of confiscation of assumed drug profits and dealers' property, in addition to criminal punishments, as well as administrative and penal sanctions against money-laundering by banks. It is, however, clear that with these measures and foreign experience so far, sweeping results can hardly be expected.

While countries like Britain, Spain, and France have sanctions against money-laundering, the most extensive are in the USA, and include restrictions on bank secrecy. Despite bank reporting of 'suspicious' cash transactions over $10,000, the US treasury estimates that $100 billion is laundered every year, with more drug profits laundered in the US than in any other country. With a financial turnover of hundreds of billions of dollars a day this is not surprising.

A study by the Max Planck Institute in Freiburg reports that no more than one per cent of the estimated profits from drug trading is identified and confiscated. Moreover, given the necessary numbers of suspects and police follow-up investigation of suspects, it is actually possible that the damages of such sanctions to civil rights, as well as economic damage to specific areas, outweigh the possible benefits.

The available methods of camouflaging drug money-laundering are many and varied. They include traditional high-level payment transactions – for art, antiques, precious metals, watches, property, casinos and bogus openings of bars, restaurants and luxurious department stores, including bringing in call-girls as front women. Other methods include phoney international import-export transactions (high invoice payments for worthless or sham deliveries), payments made to or from savings accounts in tax havens or Eastern bloc countries and from there to Western banks and over-the-counter transactions or anonymous 'havala banking', which place earnings from black market investments or shareholder's credits in open partnership corporations. These are all payments that can hardly be checked.

Sanctions are part of a major effort against drugs, but this approach begins with the results of drug crimes, that is the use of inflated black market profits. Instead we must be concerned with preventing the problem before it starts. For this, the decriminalization of drug use for personal consumption is a necessary first step.

To remove the dynamic force from the illegal drug market's long chain of dealers and its exorbitant rate of profit, there must be government or government-licensed distribution of drugs examined for quality and sold at fixed prices. Such an approach is already approved today in European social democratic and liberal circles. A prerequisite for this is the realization that criminalizing the use of certain culturally foreign drugs must be overcome by a social confrontation with the reality of addiction as a disease.

However, leeway for such reform options is now threatened by the December 1988 UN convention against trafficking in banned addictive and psychotropic substances. Unlike international agreements on this subject in 1961 and 1972, the latest treaty requires signatories to increase sanctions and use their present authority more repressively; it also restricts liberal practices such as those in the Netherlands.

For instance, punishment for the possession, cultivation and sale of all illegal drugs, including for personal use, would now have to be clearly established and enforced. Instead of abolishing such legal penalties, more and longer prison sentences are supposed to be handed down. Probation is supposed to be limited, the statutory period of limitation for prosecuting increased, and pre-trial detention required more often. This treaty was signed by the German government, but has not been ratified by the parliament. Given its repressive nature, described here only briefly, we urge the German government not to permit this agreement to take effect in West Germany.

Only through such reforms can local drug policies leave these dead-ends behind and move towards meaningful change. This means politicians must stop using the 'war on drugs' slogan as a strategy to divert attention from more urgent problems. Instead, they should begin to examine the not-so-clear differences between legal and illegal drugs. If drug addiction and the drug trade were no longer declared a sin, but rather recognized as a real disease and an economic factor that can be controlled, we would come closer to solving the problems it causes, and benefit all those affected.

Appendix 5: Ban weapons exports and strengthen export monitoring

Iraq's occupation of Kuwait revealed the responsibility of many United Nations member states for the Iraqi arms build-up. Each of the five permanent members of the Security Council as well as other industrialized and developing countries have contributed to Iraq's arsenal.

Following the collapse of the Shah's regime and the rise of Islamic fundamentalism in Iran, many Western countries believed that they should bolster and develop a regional counterpart to this threat. As a result, in the 1980s a torrent of weapons and sophisticated weapons-grade technology flooded Iraq. However, this plan has proved to be fatally wrong.

The fact that in the armed conflict between Iraq and the Western allies, weapons shipped to Iraq were turned not only against the citizens of the importing country and its neighbours but also against citizens of the exporting nations sent in as soldiers, has stimulated a new international debate around limiting weapon exports.

The international arms market

The international arms trade has always been a strictly guarded national secret – and still is. With few exceptions official statistics for this area of commerce are unavailable. The Stockholm International Peace Research Institute (SIPRI) estimates that in 1988 alone, the worldwide transfer of large weapons' systems totalled US $21 billion. Large weapon systems, however, are only part of the global arms market. ACDA statistics (which include ammunition, component parts, logistical equipment, small arms, military electronics as well as other material) estimated the overall value of international arms transfers at $48.6 billion in 1988.

Currently the USA and USSR are the leading arms exporters, followed

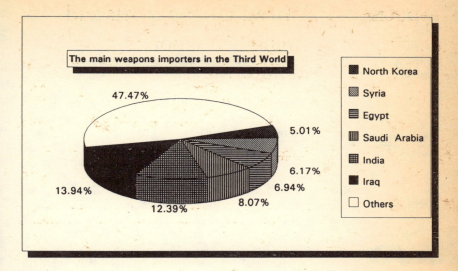

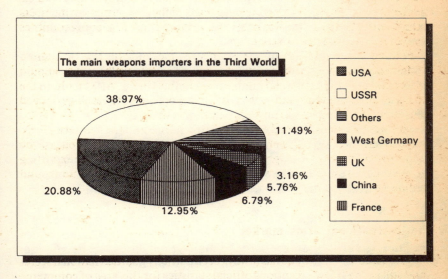

by France, Great Britain and West Germany. There have been considerable shifts on the supply side in the past decade, and the superpower suppliers face increased competition from small countries. For these countries, arms exports are a source of foreign currency rather than an instrument of foreign and defence policy. Arms, today, are marketed like any other product.

The change on the supply side has been accompanied by a change in demand. Even though 'Third World' countries have been generous customers for years, their rocketing debts have forced many of them to reduce or even cancel arms imports. This shrinking demand has caused increased competition among the suppliers. This, in turn, strengthens the bargaining power of arms importing countries. Arms exporters who cannot offer a financing package, counter-trade and/or other benefits, are hardly even considered. What was once a sellers' market has become a buyers' market.

Profitable business in Germany

Blueprints for submarines to South Africa, a chemical weapons' factory for Libya, equipment for atomic bomb construction to Pakistan and India, mycotoxins for biological weapons to Iraq, aircraft fighter planes for Jordan – the chronicle of German scandals, in part officially authorized, in part tolerated by government agencies, goes on and on.

It is impossible to confirm the exact quantities of West German arms' exports, the particular items delivered or the recipient countries. This is because of the government's policy of secrecy. German law differentiates between 'weapons of war' (*Kriegswaffen*) and arms material in general. The Weapons of War Control Act (*Kriegswaffenkontrollgesetz*, KWKG) defines 'weapons of war' as weapons, substances and organisms that are directly 'intended for war' as established by the War Weapons List (an appendix to the KWKG). Items not listed include weapons' production facilities or equipment necessary to build these facilities. Blueprints for the construction of such plants are also not included in this list. According to this delimitation the government estimates the value of war weapons' shipments in 1987 at 2.43 billion DM, for 1988 at 970 million DM. These weapons were exported to 52 countries in 1987 and 45 countries in 1988. Which countries was not revealed. SIPRI's research, however, indicates that 60 per cent of the West German arms exports go to developing countries, with more than two-thirds concentrated in five countries: Argentina, Colombia, Malaysia, Bahrain and Kuwait.

The Foreign Trade Act (*Aussenwirtschaftsgesetz*, AWG) contains a comprehensive list of weapons, ammunition and armaments whose export requires permission. Unlike the 'weapons of war' list, this one goes beyond weapons directly 'intended for war'. It includes items and facilities necessary for weapon development and production. Other items requiring export permission are contained in the atomic energy list (section B); the list of strategically important products (section C); the list of chemicals and chemical facilities (section D); and the list of biological production facilities (section E). Section D was included in the law in 1984 because of German companies' participation in the construction of poison gas plants in Iraq. Section E was included in connection with the amendment of the Foreign Trade Act after the Rabta scandal in 1989, over a German firm's sale of a chemical weapons' plant to Libya.

According to the German federal government, from 1983 to 1989, the authorized export of goods included in the lists mentioned above has the following value (in billions of DM):

	List A	List B	List C	List D	List E
1983	7.0	2.2	13.2	-	-
1984	4.1	2.1	12.8	-	-
1985	5.8	2.3	19.8	-	-
1986	5.3	2.4	17.8	-	-
1987	6.3	2.7	19.4	-	-
1988	7.0	2.8	24.3	-	-
1989	13.0	2.3	29.0	0.1	-

The legal framework: Article 26, paragraph 1 of the Federal German Constitution declares unconstitutional and punishable by law acts capable of and committed with the intention of destroying the peaceful co-existence between peoples, particularly in the case of preparations for offensive war. To aid in the implementation of this constitutional act, Article 26 established that certain weapons of war may be produced, transported and marketed only with government permission. Article 26 further states that the specific details for the implementation of this act must be regulated by federal law. It was to this end that the Weapons of War Control Act (KWKG) and the Foreign Trade Act (AWG) were passed.

Whereas the KWKG regulates the production, transport and export of 'weapons of war', the export of commodities and services in general is regulated by the Foreign Trade Act (AWG). This act empowers the federal government to enact statutory orders by which exports may be reduced or attached with special conditions according to volume, value and recipient. The lists mentioned above are constantly revised and include all products requiring special permission.

In addition to the lists of products, there is a classified list of importing countries according to the A/B and C categories. Category A/B applies to all non-communist countries, list C to communist countries. All commodities on product lists A-E need prior official export permission if their destination is a communist country (on list C).

As a result of the Rabta scandal, international pressure forced the federal government to amend legislation to prohibit the development, production and dissemination of nuclear, biological and chemical weapons. Violations are punishable by a minimum sentence of two years with no possibility of a suspended sentence or probation. A strict liability tort has been included, which would hold liable those guilty of any act that imperils the security or the foreign relations of the Federal Republic of Germany or the peaceful co-existence of peoples. German criminal law is to be applied in the case of collaboration of German citizens in the development of arms in foreign states. The authorities responsible for exercising this control have been expanded both in terms of personnel and their rights of intervention to collect and exchange data concerning suspected companies.

The government has also prepared a supplementary list of countries (list H) comprised of 53 so-called 'critical' states, mostly 'Third World'. The export of specified sensitive technologies to these countries requires prior official permission.

Despite the government's optimistic assurance that all loopholes have been closed, the Gulf War has shaken the German government's post-Rabta complacency. Iraqi missile attacks on Israel exposed the fact that German companies had helped to widen the range of Iraqi SCUD missiles. The government immediately proclaimed its intention to overhaul export regulations in order to plug the 'last remaining loopholes'. Among other measures taken, customs officials will be authorized to rescind the right of secrecy in postal and telecommunications. Falsification of export application declarations has been transformed from a misdemeanor to a crime. Violations of UN embargoes are punishable by a maximum prison sentence of up to ten years. The confiscation of profits obtained through illegal arms trade is to be facilitated and German experts' collaboration in foreign arms projects must be officially approved.

A completely 'normal' business

What is the economic and political background for the involvement of West German companies in international arms trade?

First of all, like any other commodity, weapons are produced to be sold. In this respect, tanks, bombs and other war equipment are no different from other consumer or investment goods. Arms need buyers. The German armed forces are usually a reliable source of demand. Military purchasing power is, however, insufficient to meet existing production capacities. The German arms industry sees itself confronted with a stagnating or even shrinking domestic demand for weapons. Large procurement programmes are expiring without sufficient numbers of new orders on the horizon. The situation will be further aggravated if the Vienna agreement on the reduction of conventional arms takes effect.

The declining domestic demand for arms will considerably increase the need to export. Therefore additional sales channels are sought.

In Germany, as well as in the rest of Europe, the arms industry is in the midst of a merger fever. A highpoint was the take-over of MBB (Messerschmidt, Bölkow, Blohm) in September 1989 by the Daimler-Benz (Mercedes) company. Since 1985, Daimler has gradually bought more and more arms-producing companies or shares in them: MTU (engine construction), Dornier (drones, satellites, fighter planes) and AEG (naval engineering technology, electronics). Since the take-over of MBB, Daimler is the only supplier of arms equipment in the following major markets:

Market area	Market share after merging
Fighter planes	Monopoly (100%)
Helicopters	Monopoly (100%)
Satellites	Monopoly (100%)
Drones	Monopoly (100%)
Engine construction	Market leader (over 80%)
Guided missiles	Market leader (over 60%)
Military electronics	Dominant market position (over 40%)
Naval engineering technology	Strong market position
Orbital systems	Competition discontinued
Delivery systems	Predominant market position

It is obvious that such an arms giant has an interest in the sale of its different products. Through its diverse subsidiaries the newly shaped Daimler corporation will be involved in more than 30 different transnational arms projects involving numerous foreign companies in eight different countries. It would be wrong, however, to infer from the multi-nationalization of arms production a less stringent national control. In fact, the federal government approves every single delivery of parts to a multinational arms-project.

National and international mergers in the arms industry are a clear expression of the increase in competition. Competition in conventional arms has intensified since several new suppliers from threshold countries such as Brazil, Israel, and others, have emerged on to the international arms market, hungry for a slice of the pie. To keep their market share the major Western exporters tend to offer more sophisticated equipment and know-how which (at present) cannot be offered by threshold exporters.

The foreign trade policy of the present and previous German federal governments offers another explanation for the enhanced involvement of German companies in arms exports.

About one-third of the German gross national product is earned from the export of goods and services. The federal government, the financial press and the scientific establishment all agree with the sacred creed of maximizing exports. The success of economic policies is measured by annual surplus records of the trade balance. In such a climate it is natural not to over-scrutinize export violations.

The federal government alleges that the transfer of equipment for the development and production of weapons of mass destruction has been carried out illegally and that it, itself, is the victim of unscrupulous shady characters. In reality, however, illegal arms exports are an *exception* to the rule.

Most arms shipments in the past were stamped and signed by the proper German authorities. Even when fraudulent practices were discovered, the federal government remained silent and attempted to cover up the matter as much as possible. Parliamentary investigations were crippled by the rights of the majority pro-government parties, inquiries were delayed, evidence was not considered, records were destroyed and court proceedings were abandoned for questionable reasons.

Foreign trade controls in Germany were looser than in other Western countries. Formally the government's practice finds its justification in the Foreign Trade Act. The credo of German foreign trade policy is stated in the AWG: 'Goods, services, capital, payments and economic transactions with foreign economic areas ... are fundamentally free.' Restrictions should be formed in such a way 'that the freedom of economic activity will be intruded upon as little as possible'.

The ultra-liberal foreign trade ideology of the German political and economic elite has created a certain pro-export atmosphere in the federal agencies in charge of export control. Senior officials in the Ministry of Economics and its subordinate agency, the Federal Office for the Economy (*Bundesamt für Wirtschaft*, BAW) have developed an extreme chumminess with exporters. On various occasions BAW officials have advised arms merchants how to formulate export applications.

The illegal transfer of arms could flourish only because the control authorities were completely understaffed and underfinanced. The small number of staff members prevented the effective fulfilment of the task. Only 80 of the BAW's approximately 500 civil servants worked in the foreign trade control section. Even if this small group of officials were really interested in strengthening controls, they would be doomed to failure when confronted with 18 million shipments a year. The personnel and financial situation is not accidental but rather the result of political priorities.

Even German courts have criticized the conscious negligence of control agencies. In a verdict against the supplier of nuclear technology to Pakistan, the government was rebuked for its 'failure to abide by its international obligations (including those of the non-proliferation treaty)'. In another proceeding the judge criticized the fact that controls are carried out – if at all – only half-heartedly and in the interest of trade and industry.

The Greens' demands

The Green Party has tried to inform the public through more than 100 parliamentary inquiries and motions about the government's scandalous arms export practices. The most important demands of the Green Party are:

1. An immediate and complete halt to all arms, armaments and nuclear exports: The fact that German companies contributed to the build-up of Iraq's arms arsenal has conferred new impetus for a general ban on arms exports.

The Social Democratic Party wants arms exports to be restricted to NATO member countries. Such a measure would make sense only if all NATO member states unanimously agreed on such a rule. Otherwise, German weapons manufacturers would channel their products to the country with the loosest controls, and export from there to third countries. As it is very unlikely that France and Great Britain in particular will renounce arms exports as an instrument of foreign policy, Germany should unilaterally ban arms exports.

But unilateral measures are only a 'second best' solution. To prevent the undermining of national export restrictions via exports to third countries, efforts for a general ban on arms exports should be undertaken on the EC and UN levels.

2. **Funding for a conversion program in the arms industry:** Estimates assume that in West Germany between 37,000 and 60,000 employees are dependent on arms export. A strict prohibition of arms exports will cause unemployment. Hence, alternative employment opportunities have to be developed.

Other Green demands focus on regulating arms exports and immediately strengthening the access of parliament and the public to information.

3. **Termination of all arms co-operation agreements with foreign partners for the development, production or marketing of armaments:** German companies have joined with a number of companies in other states to (co) produce arms. Some of these weapons systems have been exported to conflict areas including Iraq, Iran, Saudi Arabia, and Egypt. Though the government has accords with co-producing states that subject export to other parties to prior consultation, in no case has the government interfered; in a number of cases the government has deliberately renounced its right of intervention. This means that co-operating countries may export to any other country.

In addition, the Political Rules of the Federal Government for the Export of Weapons of War and Other Arms furnish another 'justification' for the government's conscientious ignorance. The 'Rules' hold that German end-user regulations are not applicable to co-produced weapons systems because the finished (arms) product is assumed to be of 'new origin'. The co-operating country is regarded as the end-user country.

4. **Cancellation of public guarantees for arms exports:** The involvement of German state agencies in arms exports is not just limited to checking and approving export applications; in fact, arms export is a state-subsidized matter. In order to stimulate exports in general, Germany (as well as many other states) offers the exporters a broad range of state guarantees against the importer's insolvency, and other risks. These are the so-called Hermes guarantees. That the government provides such guarantees became public knowledge through the sale of submarines to Argentina and South Korea, the export of tanks to Turkey and mine-sweepers to Saudi Arabia.

5. **Publication of all permitted arms exports:** The German government's treatment of data on arms exports is ambiguous. Within the UN they support establishment of an international register on arms exports, because the availability of reliable data is a fundamental prerequisite for disarmament. But

when asked for such data on the national level the government has refused. They perceive full public disclosure of data on arms exports as unacceptable for political reasons.

The Green Party proposed a bill to require the federal government to present a complete and detailed listing to parliament of officially permitted arms exports. The proposal was rejected by the conservative and liberal majority in the parliament.

6. Parliament must be informed of planned export approvals well ahead of time: To ensure that parliamentary committees are informed of exports before the fact, and not, as usual, through the newspaper, the Green Party demanded that the federal government inform the parliament ahead of time about export authorizations for arms. Again, the majority of the parliament did not take advantage of its right to information.

Abbreviations

AAWORD	African Association of Women for Research and Developmant
AHK	Foreign Chambers of Commerce (*Auslandshandelskammern*)
AWG	Foreign Trade Law (*Aussenwirtschaftsgesetz*)
BAK	Federal Supervision Office for Credit Systems (*Bundesaufsichtsamt für Kreditwesen*)
BIS	Bank for International Settlements
BUKO	Federal Congress of Development Policy Action Groups (*Bundeskongress Entwicklungspolitischer Aktionsgruppen*)
CCMEA	Comecon Council for Mutual Economic Assistance
CSCE	Conference on Security and Co-operation in Europe
DIHT	German Chamber of Industry and Commerce (*Deutscher Industrie- und Handelstag*)
EBRD	European Bank for Reconstruction and Development
EC	European Community = European Economic Community
ECE	Economic Commission for Europe
ECU	European Currency Unit
EEC	European Economic Community = European Community
EFTA	European Free Trade Association
ETUC	European Trade Union Confederation
FAO (UN)	Food and Agriculture Organization
GATT	General Agreement on Tariffs and Trade
GEPA	Society for the Support of Partnership with the Third World (*Gesellschaft zur Förderung der Partnerschaft mit der Dritten Welt*)
IBRD	International Bank for Reconstruction and Development (World Bank)
ICC	International Chamber of Commerce
ICFTU	International Confederation of Free Trade Unions
IDA	International Development Agency
IFC	International Finance Corporation

IHK	Chamber of Industry and Commerce (*Industrie- und Handelskammer*)
ILO	International Labour Organization
IMF	International Monetary Fund
IOCU	International Organization of Consumers' Unions
IPCC	Intergovernmental Panel for Climate Change
KWKG	Weapons of War Control Act (*Kriegswaffenkontrollgesetz*)
MIGA	Multilateral Investment Guarantee Agency
NGO	Non-Governmental Organization
NWEO	New World Economic Order
OECD	Organization for Economic Co-operation and Development
OPEC	Organization of Petroleum Exporting Countries
SEA	Single European Act
STABEX	Export Stabilization System
SYSMIN	Mining Credit System
TOES	The Other Economic Summit
TUAC	Trade Union Advisory Committee
UNCTAD	United Nations Conference on Trade and Development
UNCTC	United Nations Centre on Transnational Corporations
UNDP	United Nations Development Programme
UNESCO	United Nations Educational Scientific and Cultural Organization
UNHCR	United Nations High Commissioner for Refugees
UNICEF	United Nations Children's Fund
UNIDO	United Nations Industrial Development Organization
WHO	World Health Organization

Glossary

Bank for International Settlements (BIS)
Based in Basel. Founded in 1930 in the legal form of a joint stock company to settle German reparation payments and the debt crisis of the time. Shareholders are the central banks in Europe (excluding the USSR and Albania), Australia, Canada, Japan, South Africa and the US. Tasks: Currency co-operation between the G-10 countries; since 1973 varied functions for the handling of actions relating to the EMS and committee for bank statutes and monitoring processes.

Chamber of Industry and Commerce (IHK)
Represents the interests of the business community of a district. Public corporation. (Umbrella organization is DIHT). Tasks: representation before communal authorities; advisory services for members; specialized information services; supporter of professional education; arbitration of competition conflicts.

Conference on Security and Co-operation in Europe (CSCE)
With the 'final act' approved in Helsinki in 1975, 35 countries from Western and Eastern Europe and North America confirmed their desire to co-operate in the areas of security, economics, science, technology, the environment and humanitarian concerns, as well as the Mediterranean region. Since then regular conferences for the individual areas are held.

Council of Europe
The Council of Europe is composed of members from 21 European countries. In addition to the EC states, members are Iceland, Lichtenstein, Malta, Norway, Austria, Sweden, Switzerland, Turkey and Cyprus. The most important areas of activity are the protection of human rights (European Convention for the Protection of Human Rights and Basic Freedoms); social policies (European Codex of Social Security); environmental policies, legal policies, and cultural policies as well as regional policies. Institutions: Parliamentary Assembly and Committee of Ministers. Publications: The Council of Europe: Annual Report of the Secretary General.

Economic Commission for Europe (ECE)
Based in Geneva. This UN commission was founded in 1947, before the Cold War, to aid concerted action for the economic reconstruction of Europe after WW II. Gunnar Myrdal was first executive secretary. The ECE has 34 members in North America, Western and Eastern Europe and the Soviet Union. It compiles economic statistics on trade, industry and technology, the environment and migration. There are four further multilateral commissions for regional economic co-operation: Africa (ECA); Latin America (ECLA); Asia and the Pacific (AESCAP); and West Asia (ECWA). Publications: Economic Survey of Europe, Economic Bulletin.

Economic Commission for Latin America (ECLA)
Based in Santiago de Chile (ECE). The most strategically important development policy commission and best known UN economic commission.

European Monetary System (EMS)
Union for currency policies within the EC since 1979. All EC states are members, with special regulations for Great Britain and Greece. The goal of the EMS is the close financial and monetary co-ordination and support of European economic integration. Three elements of this system are: fixed central rates (composite exchange rates with a fixed fluctuation range); short- and medium-term credit mechanisms equalling 62 billion DM and the European Currency Unit (ECU). The ECU serves as a reference for the exchange rate mechanism; it is a mathematical unit, less important as an investment currency. The EMS is viewed overall as a successful experiment for a regional composite currency.

Federal Congress of Development Policy Action Groups (BUKO)
Umbrella organization of more than 300 West German Third World initiatives and solidarity committees founded in 1981, with headquarters in Hamburg. Focus: responsibility of the German federal government, industry and banks for neocolonial structures; the unilateral economic and political independence of developing countries. Work has included: arms campaign; agricultural co-ordination; global economics and debt; EC integration. Members of International Coalition for Development Action in Brussels (ICTA). Publications: FORUM for Development Policy Action Groups.

Foreign Chambers of Commerce (AHK)
An organization established along the lines of the IHK to support export interests. Chambers work closely with diplomatic representatives abroad. Ninety per cent of West German foreign trade in 1989 took place in the 45 countries where West German Foreign Chambers of Commerce and trade and industry representatives are active.

Group of 7 (G-7)
A committee consisting of the financial ministers and central bank executives of Canada, France, West Germany, Italy, Japan, the UK and the US. Introduced

within the framework of the IMF and under the participation of the IMF Managing Director. Co-ordination of estimates on global economic and financial trends.

Group of 10 (G-10)
The ten major industrial countries (of these Germany and Switzerland are represented by their central banks), which founded the 1962 'General Agreements to Borrow' within the framework of the IMF. GAB is an agreement for direct credit guarantees to the IMF by these countries in their own currencies. Members are the G-7, Belgium, the Netherlands, Sweden and also Switzerland (therefore there are actually 11 members). Support is provided by the IMF, BIS and OECD. G-10 holds consultative meetings on international finance questions, often with the IMF Managing Director.

Group of 24 (G-24)
A sub-group of G-77, introduced within the framework of the IMF to represent the interests of the developing countries. The group has eight members each from Africa, the Americas and Europe/Asia. Support is provided by the IMF, UNCTAD and UNDP. Regular meetings are attended by the IMF Managing Director as well as representatives of various international organizations of G-77 countries, which have observer status. G-24 has proposed various reforms of the international financial system.

Group of 77 (G-77)
An organization of 127 developing countries, aimed at reforming the global economy. Group 77 substantially contributed to the development of the ideas of the 'New World Economic Order' (NWEO). G-77 was set up to prepare for UNCTAD I in 1964 in Geneva, to develop an alternative model to the voting rights and interest relations in GATT at the UN level. The G-77 has made demands in the areas of international trade (Treaty on Raw Materials), development financing, transfer of technology, and industrialization.

International Chamber of Commerce (ICC)
Founded in 1919, based in Paris. Organization of Western corporations and corporation unions. Private organization. West Germany is represented in the ICC by the German Group of International Chambers of Commerce (IHK) seated in Cologne. Tasks: support of world trade; liberalization; harmonization of terms of trade; consultative status for the Economic and Social Council of the UN and for GATT. Chief organ is the ICC Congress, which meets every three years. Publications: ICC Business World, Annual Report, Handbook.

International Organization of Consumers' Unions (IOCU)
Umbrella organization of 174 consumer unions from 63 countries, founded in 1960. Projects are chosen in the framework of UN guidelines for consumer protection. Main areas are research and distribution of information and education. One focus is the establishment of behaviour codexes for transnational concerns.

Regular publications: IOCU Newsletter and Consumer Currents. Headquarters are located in The Hague, Penang and Montevideo.

Multilateral Investment Guarantee Agency (MIGA)
The youngest member of the World Bank group, founded in 1988. Supports investment for the economic development of its members by offering foreign investors guarantees for non-commercial losses.

Organization for Economic Cooperation and Development (OECD)
Members are: Australia; EFTA members (Finland, Iceland, Norway, Austria, Sweden, Switzerland); EC members; Japan, Canada, New Zealand, Turkey and the US; Yugoslavia has a special status. Headquarters in Paris, with permanent representation in Washington DC. The OECD emerged after 1948 from the countries that took part in the Marshall Plan. After reconstruction, the union was extended and in 1961 became the OECD, its focus also changed at this time. While the economic co-operation within Western Europe was continued by the EEC and EFTA, the OECD developed into a committee which took over the co-ordination of financial, monetary and economic policy of the industrial states. The goals of OECD include the expansion of world trade as well as growth and development supports. The OECD is a large think-tank that produces many reports, studies and statistics. The Development Assistance Committee (DAC) functions as a helper organ within the OECD. This committee discusses and makes decisions on development policy initiatives.

Programme for the Reshaping of Industrial Society
Programme of the Green Party to combat mass unemployment, poverty and environmental destruction. Immediate measures show what room for political negotiation exists at the federal level. The programme was approved by the national conference of the Green Party in September 1986 and an updated version is in preparation. The Green Party's central demands now contain a new and separate chapter based on the foreign economic policy concepts presented here for an ecological economy based on solidarity.

South Commission
Independent international commission, which was founded in Zimbabwe at the 1986 Conference of Non-Aligned Nations. The commission's task is to advise the countries of the South in solving development problems in the direction of creating a more socially just, economically functionable and ecologically healthy society. The Commission also supports South-South co-operation and in respect to North-South relations aims to increase South participation in the shaping of the world economic order. The central office is located in Geneva, the current chairman is Julius K. Nyerere, Tanzania. The South Commission is financed by voluntary contributions from Southern countries. Members of the Commission are 28 scientific, political, cultural and economic experts, three of whom are women.

STABEX
System for stabilizing raw materials exports in the framework of the Lomé Agreements.

SYSMIN
Credit system offering financial help to restructure mining companies.

The Other Economic Summit (TOES)
Since 1984 an informal union of critical scientists, politicians and grassroots' organizations, meeting parallel to the annual economic summit of the Group of Seven to discuss pressing global economic problems and formulate demands on the responsible authorities.

World Market, World Market Fixation, Maximization of Exports
In our programme we demand that world market orientation and the principle of export maximization be abandoned. For this purpose, we make use of the political and historically specific term, 'world market'. Use of this term places unequal starting positions and asymmetrically dependent relations such as those inherent in the terms 'development', 'neocolonial structures', or 'free trade' in the foreground. Viewed in purely technocratic terms, the world market comprises all commodities and service transactions that extend beyond national borders. When seen in this way, all changes in national borders also mean a shift in world market conditions. For example, the creation of the EC, as well as German reunification, reduce the size of the world market without changing the structures of world market orientation.

The group of Green economists

Dieter Bricke (born 1932)
Group co-ordinator and 'coach'. Doctoral degree in economics (Manpower Planning in India – Conflicts between Social Policy and Economic Growth). 1965-68 Director, German Volunteer Service (DED) in India and Nepal. 1968-74 Managing Director Kuebel-Foundation, Bensheim. Since 1974 Senior Officer, German Foreign Office. 1986-89 seconded advisor to the Parliamentary Group of the Green Party in Bonn. Special interests: international trade, world market reforms and ethics in economics.

Claudia Dziobek (born 1956)
Ph.D in economics (studied in Paris, Freiburg and Amherst, Massachusetts). 1984-86 researcher and lecturer, Free University of Berlin, J. F. Kennedy Institute. 1986-91 staff economist, Parliamentary Group of the Green Party in Bonn. Special Interests: Banking, international finance and industrial policy. 1988-90 Member of the advisory board to the Ökobank in Frankfurt. 1991-92 engaged in a university research project on European bank regulation, and guest scholar at the Brookings Institute in Washington DC.

Thomas Fues (born 1952)
Economist (studied in Bonn and at the Massachusetts Institute of Technology, MIT). 1980-83 staff economist, German Development Institute (DIE) Berlin. 1983-90 staff economist, Parliamentary Group of the Green Party, Bonn. Special interests: development policy, international trade and human rights. Since then, working at home raising children and as free-lance consultant. Board member of WEED (World Economy, Ecology and Development), a Bonn-based non-governmental organization.

Michael Hadamczik (born 1951)
Economist (studied in Frankfurt). Journalist and editor for a national magazine on ecological consumption. Since 1988 staff economist for the Green Parliamentary Group in the Deutsche Bundestag. Special interests: European economic and political integration; East-West co-operation.

Frithjof Schmidt (born 1953)
Doctoral degree in social science studies (Bochum University). Founding member and chairperson of the South-East Asian Information Centre in Bochum. 1988-89 staff researcher/advisor, Parliamentary Group of the Green Party, Bonn. Since 1989, administrative officer, the Greens in the European Parliament.

Peter Sellin (born 1949)
Economist (Free University of Berlin). Teacher at a Berlin community college for economics, social and legal studies. Founding member of the German Green Party and of the Alternative Liste in Berlin in 1980. Member of the Berlin Parliament (1981-83) and Member of Parliament in the Bundestag, Bonn (1987-89). Special interests: CSCE, Economic Ecology of East-West European Integration.

Eckhard Stratmann-Mertens (born 1948)
Secondary school teacher of political science, history and Protestant theology (studied in Tübingen, Munich, Frankfurt) 1977-83. Founding member of the Green Party. Member of Parliament in the Bundestag 1983-85 and 1987-90. Special interests: energy policy. Since 1991 founding member and member of staff of the Institute for Ecological Regional Development in the Ruhrgebiet.

Barbara Unmuessig (born 1956)
Political scientist (Free University of Berlin). 1983-85 Publisher and editor of a well-known Third World magazine (*iz3W*) in Freiburg. 1985-90 staff researcher/advisor to the Parliamentary Group of the Green Party, Bonn. Special interests: international environmental issues, multilateral banking and development. Founding member of WEED in Bonn (1989) and co-publisher of the information letter 'World Economy and Development'. Co-ordinator of UNCED-92 for German non-governmental organizations.

Ludger Volmer (born 1952)
Social scientist (studied sociology, social psychology and political science at Bochum University). 1979-83 empirical analyst for the regional planning board in the Ruhr Valley. Founding member of the Green Party. 1983-85 staff researcher for the Green Parliamentary Group. 1985-90 Member of Parliament, Green Parliamentary Group, Bundestag committees on economic co-operation and foreign policy. Special interests: Development finance; interaction between parliament and non-government organizations. 1991 Speaker of the German Green Party.

Index